The CREAM BOOK

SENTENCE SERMONS

Sentences That Stick
for
Sermons
Bible Lessons
Talks and Testimonies

*Arranged by Topics
in Alphabetical Order*

Compiled by
KEITH L. BROOKS

MOODY PRESS • CHICAGO

ISBN: 0-8024-0117-1

Printed in the United States of America

TOPICS

Affliction
Anger
Appreciation
Bible
Cheerfulness
Church
Conceit
Conscience
Consecration
Courtesy
Diligence
Faith
Faithfulness
Forgiveness
Friendship
Generosity
Heaven
Hell
Home
Honesty
Humility
Hypocrisy
Influence
Intemperance
Knowledge
Love
Lying

Marriage
Meditation
Missions
Opportunity
Peace
Praise to God
Prayer
Preaching
Providence
Repentance
Reputation
Righteousness
Salvation
Second Coming of Christ
Self-denial
Self-righteousness
Service for Christ
Sin
Skepticism
Soul-winning
Speech
Success
Temptation
Today
Worldliness
Worry
Worship

CROSS-REFERENCE INDEX

Adoration. *See* Worship

Adversity. *See* Affliction

Agreeableness. *See* Cheerfulness

Anxiety. *See* Worry

Atheism. *See* Skepticism

Belief. *See* Faith

Bible Study. *See* Meditation

Bitterness. *See* Anger

Boasting. *See* Conceit

Character. *See* Righteousness

Cheating. *See* Honesty

Christlikeness. *See* Righteousness

Circumstances. *See* Providence

Comfort. *See* Affliction

Commendation. *See* Appreciation

Communion. *See* Worship

Companions. *See* Worldliness

Complaining. *See* Worry

Confessing Christ. *See* Soul-winning

Consolation. *See* Affliction

Contrition. *See* Repentance

Conversion. *See* Salvation

Conviction. *See* Conscience

Courage. *See* Faithfulness

Covetousness. *See* Generosity

Cowardice. *See* Faithfulness

Criticism. *See* Speech

Cross-bearing. *See* Self-denial

Deceit. *See* Lying

Discouragement. *See* Worry

Dishonesty. *See* Honesty

Doubt. *See* Skepticism

Education. *See* Knowledge

Efficiency. *See* Service

Evangelism. *See* Missions, Soul-winning

Example. *See* Influence

Failure. *See* Success

Falsehood. *See* Lying

5

CROSS-REFERENCE INDEX (Cont.)

False Pride. *See* Conceit
Fear. *See* Worry
Fidelity. *See* Faithfulness
Fools. *See* Knowledge
Forbearance. *See* Love
Formalism. *See* Hypocrisy
Fruit-bearing. *See* Service
Future Retribution. *See* Hell

Gentleness. *See* Courtesy
Giving. *See* Generosity
Godliness. *See* Righteousness
Gratitude. *See* Praise
Guidance. *See* Consecration.

Happiness. *See* Cheerfulness
Heresy. *See* Skepticism
Holiness. *See* Righteousness
House of God. *See* Church

Idleness. *See* Diligence
Impurity. *See* Sin
Inconsistency. *See* Hypocrisy
Indecency. *See* Sin
Industriousness. *See* Diligence
Infidelity. *See* Skepticism

Iniquity. *See* Sin
Integrity. *See* Honesty
Intercession. *See* Prayer

Joy. *See* Cheerfulness.
Judging. *See* Speech

Kindness. *See* Love

Laughter. *See* Cheerfulness
Laziness. *See* Diligence
Learning. *See* Knowledge
Luck. *See* Providence

Matrimony. *See* Marriage
Meekness. *See* Humility
Melancholy. *See* Worry
Ministers. *See* Preaching
Morality. *See* Self-righteousness
Mercy. *See* Love

Obedience. *See* Consecration
Optimism. *See* Cheerfulness

Patience. *See* Love
Penitence. *See* Repentance
Perdition. *See* Hell
Pessimism. *See* Worry
Politeness. *See* Courtesy
Pride. *See* Conceit
Progress. *See* Success
Punctuality. *See* Today

Purity. *See* Righteousness

Purpose. *See* Faithfulness

Quietude. *See* Peace

Rationalism. *See* Skepticism

Reformation. *See* Self-righteousness

Regeneration. *See* Salvation

Responsibility. *See* Opportunity

Retribution *See* Hell

Revenge. *See* Anger

Reverence. *See* Worship

Sanctification. *See* Righteousness

Scandal. *See* Speech

Scriptures. *See* Bible

Self-centered. *See* Conceit

Slander. *See* Speech

Sorrow. *See* Affliction

Spirituality. *See* Consecration

Steadfastness. *See* Faithfulness

Stinginess. *See* Generosity

Study. *See* Meditation

Submission. *See* Consecration

Suffering. *See* Affliction

Supplication. *See* Prayer

Talking. *See* Speech

Teaching. *See* Preaching

Temper. *See* Anger

Temperance. *See* Intemperance

Testimony. *See* Soul-winning

Testing. *See* Affliction

Thanksgiving. *See* Praise

Time. *See* Today

Tithing. *See* Generosity

Will of God. *See* Consecration

Trial. *See* Affliction

Trouble. *See* Affliction

Trust. *See* Faith

Unbelief. *See* Skepticism

Unrighteousness. *See* Sin

Wealth. *See* Generosity

Will of God. *See* Consecration

Wisdom. *See* Knowledge

Witnessing. *See* Soul-winning

Word of God. *See* Bible

Works. *See* Service

Yieldedness. *See* Consecration

AFFLICTION

**Adversity - Comfort - Consolation - Sorrow
Suffering - Testing - Trial - Trouble**

No Christian need have a Gethsemane without a comforting angel.

Much depends on the way we come into trouble. Paul and Jonah were both in a storm, but the circumstances were quite different.

God would have no furnaces if there were no gold to separate from the dross.

God is not only a present help in time of trouble but a great help in keeping us out of trouble.

All great souls have attended the School of Hard Knocks.

When God would give an especially bright crown to a soul, He first imparts an equally heavy cross.

Darkness cannot put out the lamp: it can only make it brighter.

Do you believe in the sun when it is hidden behind a cloud? Then doubt not the goodness of God when He seems to hide His face.

Affliction is to the people of God as the pruning knife is to the vine to prepare for greater fruitfulness.

If trial makes us impatient, then the devil laughs and is glad.

If God numbers our hairs, will He not also number our tears?

One of the greatest evidences of God's love to those who love Him is to send them afflictions with grace to bear them.

There's a tremendous difference between suffering with Christ and suffering because of wrongdoing.

Keep your face always toward the sunshine and the shadows will fall behind.

Grace teaches us in the midst of life's greatest comforts to be willing to die, and in the midst of its greatest crosses to be willing to live.

God's worst is better than the devil's best.

Your prospects are as bright as the promises of God.

Trial is the school of trust.

The gem cannot be polished without friction, nor the child of God perfected without adversity.

The Christian is a man whom God has under treatment.

If our circumstances find us in God, we shall find God in all our circumstances.

Many men owe the grandeur of their lives to their tremendous difficulties.

The world has been enriched more by the poverty of its saints than by the wealth of its millionaires.

The great Physician never takes down the wrong bottle.

Make friends with your trials as though you were going to live together always.

Sore distress is a blessing in disguise if it drives us to the power of faith and prayer.

For great missions, the preparation is great trials.

When you try to carry your burdens without God's help, you disappoint Him.

AFFLICTION (Cont.)

God tells us to burden Him with what burdens us.

Christians are like tea: their real strength is not drawn out until they get into hot water.

Into each life some rain must fall, but do not magnify each shower into a cloudburst.

Turn care into prayer.

The very thing Satan throws into our path to check us may be made the stepping-stone to higher experiences.

Be more desirous of meeting God in your trouble than of getting out of it.

Some things may come to us in rough wrappings, but there is gold inside.

Where souls are being tried and ripened, there God is hewing out pillars for His temple.

Trial affords the greatest opportunity to witness for Christ by example.

All the troubles of a Christian do but draw him nearer heaven.

The blow at the outward man may be the greatest blessing to the inward man.

Even Satan may be God's servant to make saints of us.

The eagle that soars near the sun is not concerned how it will cross the stream.

Fair-weather crews often desert when the winds begin to blow.

A puff of wind sets a shallow pond in wavelets.

Nothing will show more accurately what we are than the way in which we meet trials and difficulties.

11

AFFLICTION (Cont.)

Fellowship in Christ's suffering is the qualification for sharing in His dignity.

A black cloud makes a traveler mend his pace and mind his home.

When God sends a man to the lion's den, He goes there with him.

Great men are generally prepared for great deeds by great trials.

No gall, no glory; no cross, no crown.

Men who do not like to be put upon the grindstone are dull tools for the purposes for which God designs to use them.

We see new panoramas through our tears. Our sorrows prove the occasion of our visions.

Be sure if God sends you on stony paths, He will provide you with strong shoes.

The school of suffering graduates rare scholars.

To have suffered much is like knowing many languages: it gives the sufferer access to many more people.

The present circumstance which presses so hard against you is the best shaped tool in the Father's hand to chisel you for eternity.

God's choicest plants often live in the shade.

It is sad when our troubles try us more than our transgressions.

There are some troubles that are not cured by a Bible and hymn book. They require perspiration and a breath of fresh air.

Sorrow is only one of the lower notes in the oratorio of our blessedness.

Unstoked furnaces are for little faith; the greatest compliment God can pay us is to heat the furnace to the utmost.

There is nothing the body suffers which the soul may not profit by.

It lightens the stroke to draw near to Him who handles the rod.

Sanctified afflictions are spiritual promotions.

We go from strength to strength because we go from struggle to struggle.

The quickest cure for grief is action.

It sometimes takes rough tools to remove the rust from our hearts.

Life without its shadows is life without its grace.

Examine many of your troubles and you'll find your own name stamped on them as the manufacturer.

The devil often grinds the tools with which God works.

No one honestly can use his illness as an excuse for ineffectualness or failure.

Pain is neither a blessing nor a curse; it is an opportunity.

You'll not understand pain until you understand that life is not a pursuit of happiness, a search for ease, but is a training for greatness.

The heroes of history have not emerged from brilliantly lighted halls of luxury and self-indulgence, but from the darkened byways of suffering and persecution.

Great sufferers do the world's work. The crown of loftiest achievement is a crown of thorns.

God does not comfort us to make us comfortable · but to make us comforters.

ANGER

Bitterness - Revenge - Temper

Ecc(o2) The way to be angry and not sin, is to be angry, as Christ was, at nothing but sin.

The man who cannot be angry at evil lacks enthusiasm for good.

Men say they are not themselves when anger gets the best of them, betraying what they really are.

In taking revenge, a man is but even with his enemy. In passing it over, he is superior; for it is a prince's part to pardon.

The man who harbors ill-will against another has fast closed the ear of God against his own cry.

Out of ten times you give vent to what you consider justifiable anger, you will be sorry for nine and a half things you did. Of the remaining half, you will not be one bit proud.

He who cannot control himself is certainly unfit to control others.

Throw mud and you will have dirty hands, whether or not the mud hits the mark.

Two things we should never be angry at: the things we can't help and the things we can help.

14

ANGER (Cont.)

It costs a heap more to revenge injuries than to bear them.

Ecc(03) He invites future injuries who revenges past ones.

Ecc(oz) When a man's temper gets the best of him, it reveals the worst of him.

Never waste a minute thinking about your enemies.

When one will not quarrel, two cannot.

The most glorious victory over an enemy is to turn him into a friend.

As long as vengeance would seem sweet, self is not dead.

It is easy to give another a "piece of your mind"; but when you are through, you have lost your peace of mind.

Never take a pen in hand while there is a feeling of anger in the heart.

He is happy whose circumstances suit his temper, but he is more excellent who can suit his temper to his circumstances.

Anger is implanted within us as a sort of sting to make us gnash with our teeth against the devil, not to set us in array against each other.

The man who recognizes the fittest moment to crush his enemy and neglects it, deserves to be a conqueror.

Anger is a gun that bursts at the breach and kills the holder.

He who overcomes by force has overcome but half his foe.

ANGER (Cont.)

The best sort of revenge is not to be like him who did the injury.

It is a great thing to down your critics without saying a word and add to your friends by holding your peace.

What no gentleman should say, no gentleman need answer.

Don't permit your feelings to be hurt: that is only a form of egotism.

It often shows a fine command of language to keep still.

Many a man has found that throwing mud is ground lost.

A mule makes no headway while he's kicking; neither does a man.

A temperate anger has virtue in it.

Anger manages everything badly.

The fellow who keeps cool, commands everybody.

Men make up in wrath what they lack in reason.

Anger begins in folly and ends in repentance.

Count ten before you speak; and if you're very angry, a hundred.

When a man is wrong and won't admit it, he always gets mad.

To get angry is to revenge the fault of others upon ourselves.

Violence in the voice is usually the death-rattle of reason.

ANGER (Cont.)

The angriest person in a controversy is usually the one who is wrong.

Anger turns the mind out of doors and bolts the door.

The "last word" is the most dangerous of infernal machines.

Shallow minds, like shallow waters, are easily ruffled.

Enter into no controversy without necessity, without understanding, and without love.

APPRECIATION

Commendation of Others

The way of this world is to praise the dead saints and persecute the living ones.

He who merits praise he never receives is better off than he who receives praise he never merits.

It is a sign of a good man if he grows better for commendation.

There is as much greatness in owning a good deed as in doing it.

Flowers on the coffin shed no fragrance backward over the weary way by which a man has traveled.

It is not until a man gets nearly to the top that the world is willing to give him a boost.

Dumb gratitude is acceptable only from the dumb.

Often those of whom we speak least on earth are best known in heaven.

APPRECIATION (Cont.)

He is incapable of a truly good action who has no pleasure in praising good actions in others.

Praise is a debt we owe to the virtues of others.

The refusal of praise is only the wish to be praised twice.

Commendation from an enemy smells of craft.

Just praise is a debt but flattery is a present.

Those who are greedy of commendation prove they are short in merit.

When you receive praise of men, return it to God, the blesser of the action.

Sweet is the breath of praise when given by those whose own high merit claims the praise they give.

Sincere praise is the most powerful excitement to commendable actions.

Judicious commendation is to children what the sun is to flowers.

BIBLE

Scriptures - Word of God

Ecc(03)
The Bible is the sheet anchor of our liberties. Write its principles upon your heart and practice them in your lives. *U. S. Grant.*

Man could not have written the Bible if he would and would not if he could. *John Wesley.*

There is not a shaft in the quiver of the devil but has been fired at the Bible and failed.

18

BIBLE (Cont.)

The Bible is the one window of hope in this prison through which we look into eternity.

When Jesus speaks, let fallible mortals hold their peace. *John E. Godbey.*

We may tremble on the Rock of Ages, but the Rock will never tremble under us. *John MacNeill.*

Ecclo3 If a man is not familiar with the Bible, he has suffered a loss which he had better make all possible haste to correct. *Theodore Roosevelt.*

The Bible is the only Book for thinkers, readers, scholars, speakers, men, women, children. If we can have only one Book, save us that! *J. H. Choate.*

Eccl8 Here is a Book, the Bible, worth more than all others that were ever printed; yet it is my misfortune never to have found time to read it. *Patrick Henry, near death.*

Bad men or devils would not have written the Bible, for it condemns them and their work. Good men or angels could not have written it, for in saying that it was from God when it was their own invention, they would have been guilty of falsehood and could not have been good. The only remaining Being who could have written it is God. *John Flavel.*

The only objection against the Bible is a bad life. *Wilmont, an infidel, dying.*

Ecc(p3) If there is anything in my style or thoughts to be commended, the credit is due to my kind parents, who instilled into my mind an early love for the Scriptures. *Daniel Webster.*

There are no songs comparable to the songs of Zion; no orations equal to those of the prophets; no politics like those which the Scriptures teach. *John Milton.*

BIBLE (Cont.)

England has two books, the Bible and Shakespeare. England made Shakespeare, but the Bible made England. *Victor Hugo.*

If I am asked to name the one comfort in sorrow, the safe rule of conduct, the true guide of life, I must point to what, in the words of a popular hymn, is called "the old, old story" told in an old Book, God's best and richest gift to mankind. *Wm. E. Gladstone.*

The Bible is a Book, in comparison with which all others in my eyes are of minor importance, and which, in all my perplexities and distresses, has never failed to give me light and strength. *Robert E. Lee.*

The New Testament is the best Book the world has ever known or ever will know. *Charles Dickens.*

Young man, my advice is that you cultivate an acquaintance with and a firm belief in the Scriptures, for this is your certain interest. *Benjamin Franklin.*

I have said, and always will say, that the studious perusal of the sacred Volume will make better citizens, better fathers and better husbands. *Thomas Jefferson.*

If the Bible is not the true religion, one is very excusable in being deceived; for everything in it is grand and worthy of God. The more I consider the gospel, the more I am assured there is nothing there which is not beyond the march of events and above the human mind. *Napoleon Bonaparte.*

To the Bible men will return because they cannot do without it. The true God is and must be pre-eminently the God of the Bible. *Matthew Arnold.*

The Bible is the revelation of the meaning of life, the nature of God, and the spiritual nature and needs of men. It is the only guide of life which leads the spirit in the way of peace and salvation. *Woodrow Wilson.*

The promises of the Bible have behind them God's knowledge and power. *John Wannamaker.*

One of the evidences of the inspiration and infallibility of the Word of God is that it has survived the fanaticism of its friends.

I entreat my children to maintain and defend at all hazards and at any cost of personal sacrifice the blessed doctrine of the complete atonement for sins through the blood of Jesus Christ once offered, and through that alone. *From will of J. Pierpont Morgan.*

Until our teaching is right, our life must be wrong. We must have the pure bread, pure water, the undefiled Bible. Out of such nutritious food there will come proper results, such as fellowship, sacramental communion and common prayer. *Joseph Parker.*

The Bible is certainly the best preparation that you can give a soldier going into battle, to sustain his ideal and faith. *Marshall Foch.*

The Bible is the only Book that always finds me. *Samuel T. Coleridge.*

Out of the babel of tongues now in the world, all history proves that the only salvation for the individual or the nation, is the knowledge of the obedience to the revealed Word of God. *Marshall, Vice President U. S.*

If I were to have my way, I would take the torch out of the hand of the Statue of Liberty and in its stead place an open Bible. *Marshall.*

I have always believed in the inspiration of the Holy Scriptures whereby they have become the expression to man of the word and will of God. No book of any kind ever written has ever so affected the whole life of a people. *Warren G. Harding.*

BIBLE (Cont.)

The Bible is the Word of life. I beg that you will read it and find this out for yourselves. Read not little snatches here and there but long passages that will be the road to the heart of it. *Woodrow Wilson.*

CHEERFULNESS

Agreeableness - Happiness - Joy
Laughter - Optimism

Cheerfulness greases the axles of the world.

Of all the things you wear, your expression is the most important.

No true happiness apart from holiness: no holiness apart from Christ.

Ecc(œ) Joy is the by-product of obedience to God.

Keep your happiness in circulation.

What you laugh at tells plainer than words what you are.

While seeking happiness for others, we unconsciously find it for ourselves.

You may hope for the best if you are prepared for the worst.

All the world is a camera: look pleasant please!

Better associate with a cheerful idiot than a sour-pickle sage.

Of all the lights you carry in your face, joy carries the farthest out to sea.

Salvation was never designed to make our pleasures less.

CHEERFULNESS (Cont.)

God always makes round faces. We are the ones who make long faces.

− Nothing but sin can take away the Christian's joy.

Happiness lives next door to a complete acquiescence to the will of God.

God loves a cheerful doer as well as a cheerful giver.

Grief can take care of itself; but to get the full value of joy, you must have somebody to divide it with. *Mark Twain.*

Remember, you are not only the salt of the earth but the sugar.

It is not *where* we are but *what* we are that makes our happiness.

The devil would rather put a long face on a saint than throw down a high church steeple.

Hope for the best; get ready for the worst; take cheerfully what God chooses to send.

When the Christian can carve contentment out of God's providence, whatever the dish that is set before him—that is godliness in triumph.

Unhappiness is the hunger to get. True happiness is the hunger to give.

Merely to share another's burden is noble. To do it cheerfully is sublime.

A saint needs no halo about his head, but he should have a solo in his heart.

If you can't see the bright side of a thing, then polish the dull side.

The absence of cheerfulness is a vice.

CHEERFULNESS (Cont.)

The most manifest sign of wisdom is continued cheerfulness.

If good people would but make their goodness agreeable, it would win many to the good cause.

Cheerfulness charms us with a spell that reaches into eternity.

As they grow older, human beings acquire faces they deserve.

CHURCH

There is nothing more pitiable than a soulless, sapless, shriveled church, rooted in barren professions and bearing no fruit for Christ.

The church is not a select circle for the immaculate, but a home where the outcast may come in.

Don't place upon the stranger the responsiblity of getting acquainted with you at your church.

What preacher can get inspiration looking into a lopsided aggregation of feathers, ribbons, beads, sticks, straws, corn tassles, and thistledown on the heads of the women of the congregation!

Some people devote all of their religion to going to church.

Many are in that uncertain state of health that makes them too frail to go to church on Sunday morning but just well enough to go for a joy ride Sunday afternoon.

The devil has little to fear from the spiritual activities generated in a poorly ventilated church.

CHURCH (Cont.)

The best remedy for a sick church is to put it on a missionary diet.

A man who detests the church ought to go to church at least once a year to make sure that the church has not mended the faults of which he complains.

There is no pew so vacant as the one without a spiritual worshiper.

Your own church steeple is not the only one that points to heaven.

The less real religion a church has, the more bazaars and entertainments it takes to keep it running.

The business of the church is not to furnish hammocks for the lazy but yokes for the drawing of loads.

A complacent church is a church on ice. An evangelistic church is a church on fire.

Satan has reserved a seat in many a sanctuary.

The church is not a refrigerator for perishable piety but a dynamo for charging men.

Judging from church attendance, heaven won't be packed with men.

There are many church officers who need to be fired—not out but up.

A church made up of unconverted members is a trapdoor to hell.

Let none be led away by the foolish fantasy that they can have church at home and dispense with the joy of kindred sympathy of soul.

The key that unlocks heaven doesn't fit every church door.

CHURCH (Cont.)

God's house is a hive for workers, not a nest for drones.

The prayer closets of God's people are where the roots of the church grow.

God put the church in the world. The devil put the world in the church.

Religious differences are not nearly so disastrous as religious indifferences.

The church needs less block and more tackle.

The church had never such influence over the world as in those days when she had nothing to do with the world.

The way to preserve the peace of the church is to preserve the purity of it.

It is the early bird who gets the back seat.

CONCEIT

Boasting - False Pride - Self-centered Pride

A conceited man is like a man up in a balloon: everybody looks small to him and he grows smaller to everyone else.

God can't use some people because they are so great.

Dignity is what some people stand on when they are short.

The self-satisfied can be of no service to God.

Pride often builds the nest in which poverty hatches out its sorrows.

26

CONCEIT (Cont.)

The younger the practitioner of any profession, the wiser his look.

A fool may have a knowing look, but it falls off when he opens his mouth.

Some men are like a toy balloon: a pin prick and there is nothing left of them.

If we feel we are bigger than our place, it is likely that we are thinking more of ourselves than God thinks of us.

Some look great and are not. Some are not great and look what they are. Some are great and without effort to look it.

He that would never look upon an ass must lock his door and break the looking glass.

We deem those men most remarkable who think as we do.

He who pitches too high won't get through his song.

Some people get their promotion, but they rattle around in it.

He who boasts of what his own hands have done mortgages his prosperity to the devil.

One of the worst things in the world is to be brought out of wretchedness in self to be satisfied in self.

If you want to know how important you are in the world, stick your finger in a pan of water and see the hole that is left when you take it out again.

A puny mind courts notoriety to advertise itself.

Know that the love of thyself doth hurt still more than anything else in the world.

CONCEIT (Cont.)

He is not the best carpenter who makes the most chips.

We die by living to ourselves; we live by dying to ourselves.

The "big head" is an affliction of the upper part of the skull caused by feeding conceit into a vacuum.

You get some people's *goat* by putting on the *dog*.

Pride is at the root of most of the *I can'ts* that come from Christians.

There is one good feature about the folks who are forever talking about themselves: they don't have time to talk about others.

Narrow-souled people are like narrow-necked bottles. The less they have in them the more noise they make in pouring it out.

You can always tell a man of no importance by the way he stretches his neck to get in a group photograph.

It may be all right to put up a bluff, but be careful you don't fall over it.

There are two kinds of men: the self-made ones and those who have to listen.

Pride hides a man's faults to himself and magnifies them to everyone else.

The only exercise some people get is throwing bouquets at themselves.

He who deems himself worthy of great favors should take an inventory.

Many a one-cylinder man drives an eight-cylinder car.

CONCEIT (Cont.)

It is no sign you have reached the top because you feel above your job.

Beware of the man who knows it all, especially if it be yourself.

A bold front often indicates a weak back.

The man who has the real thing is no bluffer.

If you want to please the devil, begin to admire yourself.

The fellow who considers himself a big gun is pretty sure to be fired.

An egotist is an "I" specialist.

The benches in the park are filled with men who tried to tell the boss how to run his business.

The sure way to freeze to death is to be wrapped up in yourself.

An empty man is full of himself.

The head never begins to swell until the mind stops growing.

A flea and an elephant crossed a bridge. Said the flea: "Boy, we sure did shake that thing."

When some men discharge an obligation you can hear the report for miles around.

To be a slave to one's self is the heaviest of all servitudes.

The selfish man, like a ball of twine, is wrapped up in himself.

Some people are proud of their humility.

Spiritual pride is the most arrogant of all brands of pride.

CONCEIT (Cont.)

Conceit may puff a man up, but it will never prop him up.

As one rises in real worth of character, he sinks in the scale of self-conceit.

Some men are so conceited that they never fail on their birthdays to send a telegram of congratulation to their mothers for having given them birth.

Some people are all front door, but when you open the door, you're in the background.

When you see a person's name scratched upon a glass, you know he owns a diamond and his father owns an ass.

Little bantams are great at crowing.

Nothing is done beautifully which is done in pride.

To be ever seeking the praises of men is to be consuming an opiate which will benumb the highest powers and make the soul insensible to the reproach of God.

He who swims securely down the stream of self-confidence is in danger of being drowned in the whirlpool of self-presumption.

Many a man tarnishes his victories by the way in which he displays them.

There is nothing more pitiful than a life spent in thinking of nothing but self.

Christ sends none away empty but those who are full of themselves.

Many are deaf to counsel who are open to flattery.

When a man is wrapped up in himself he makes a pretty small parcel.

CONCEIT (Cont.)

"God made two great lights," says the *Cumberland Presbyterian*, "and some people act as if they thought they are one of them."

CONSCIENCE

Conviction

Conscience is like a sundial. When the truth of God shines on it, it points the right way.

With many, conscience is the fear of being found out.

An opinion is something we pick up and carry around. A conscientious conviction is something that picks us up and carries us around.

Some men pride themselves on being true to conscience, but they are careful to see to it that conscience is under their personal control.

A quiet conscience sleeps in thunder.

The devil is forever convicting folks of other peoples' sins. The Holy Spirit convicts us of our own.

A guilty conscience needs no accusing.

Galled horses cannot endure the comb.

If conscience smites thee once, it is an admonition; if twice, it is condemnation.

Conscience is a still, small voice; and half the time when it tries to speak up, it finds that the line is busy.

Sometimes a man with a clear conscience only has a poor memory.

CONSCIENCE (Cont.)

Conscience is an inner voice that warns us some-one is looking. *Henry L. Mencken.*

A bad conscience embitters the sweetest comforts, but a good conscience sweetens the bitterest crosses.

A gash in the conscience may disfigure a soul forever.

There was a man so deaf that he could hear the voice of conscience only with difficulty.

No evil is intolerable by a guilty conscience.

Trust that man in nothing who has not conscience in everything.

A good conscience is the looking glass of heaven.

The tribunal of conscience exists independent of edicts and decrees.

Happy is the man who renounces everything that may bring a burden upon his conscience.

CONSECRATION

Guidance - Obedience - Spirituality
Submission - Will of God - Yieldedness

Those who see God's hand in everything, can best leave everything in God's hands.

One day in which the will is yielded to Him is worth a hundred of toiling in self-will.

He who makes God first will find God with him to the last.

The way to see farther ahead is to go ahead in the will of God as far as you can see.

CONSECRATION (Cont.)

You cannot give to the world any more than you give God.

God can work wonders when He can get a surrendered man to work through.

Self-will must die, and Jesus has prepared a place for it to breathe its last—at the cross.

What we have in our hand, we will lose; but what we put into God's hand is still and ever will be in our possession.

He who abandons himself to God will never be abandoned by God.

The Lord has more need of our weakness than our strength.

Christ isn't valued at all unless He is valued above all.

Make your own will as nothing before God and He will make the wills of other men as nothing before you.

When God bolts the door, don't try to get in through a window.

We need not only a constant going to do His will, but a constant tarrying to find out His will.

We often go wrong by debating with God instead of waiting on God.

The secret of an unsatisfied life lies in an unsurrendered will.

There are no disappointments to those whose wills are buried in the will of God.

Only when we die to all about us do we live to God above us.

CONSECRATION (Cont.)

If God has called you, don't spend time looking over your shoulder to see who is following you.

If we want an increase of Christ, there must be a decrease of self.

The minute we begin to unload, the Lord begins to fill in.

If your all is in the Lord's hand, why bother about what "they say?"

If you do not crown Jesus Lord of all, you really do not crown Him at all.

There never was a religion so dangerous to go half way with as Christianity.

People sometimes think they have a strong will, when it's a strong *won't*.

We must lay self aside or God will lay us aside.

There is no risk in abandoning ourselves to God.

The only way to do what we cannot do, is to let Christ do it through us.

If God has made your program, He will carry it out.

When the way seems blocked, use the blocks to mount on.

One of the most common mistakes is to mistake our wish for His will.

Emptiness is the cup into which God puts blessing.

When a door slams behind you, look for the one God is opening before you.

It does not take great men to do great things: it only takes consecrated men.

CONSECRATION (Cont.)

Consecration means to be, to do, and to suffer the will of God.

Difficulties and distresses are no indication that you are out of the path of His will. They may be a hint that you should put into your work more wit, wisdom, and warm work.

Don't expect the Lord to write an appendix to a volume about which He has not been consulted.

If you are in God's line, God will bring things in line with you.

If you would have God's guidance, you must make spiritual things your main business.

We may test our growth in grace by our expertness in detecting the voice of the Spirit.

The tasks are not too many, the hours are not too short for the doing of God's will.

When our business is to do the will of God, He will take care of the business.

There is no thought that more transforms a man's life than the thought that he can tie up his life to the doing of the will of the Almighty.

The secret of the Lord is imparted to those who have no secrets from Him.

Patient waiting is often the highest way of doing God's will.

The shortest way is not always right, nor the smoothest the safest; therefore, be not surprised if the Lord choose the farthest and roughest. But be sure of this: He will choose the best.

God's clock keeps perfect time though it may not be our time.

CONSECRATION (Cont.)

There is no way of knowing reality in Christian experience except by letting God into the details of everyday life.

The Holy Spirit flows through yielded men, not machinery.

He who brings in the Holy Spirit as his resource has already won the victory.

Many who sing, "Fill me now," might better sing, "Empty me now."

It is easier to build temples of stone than to be temples of the Holy Spirit.

The greatest barrier between some Christians and the omnipotent strength of God is their own strength.

When our capability is of God, we will never be incapable.

God calls for those who have no might nor power but yearn to be filled with His power.

Power is the twin sister of purity. Some think they want more power, when it is purity they need.

God's treasure house is only unlocked to the believer by the golden key of obedience.

Delayed obedience is the brother of disobedience.

The hidden things of God are not discovered until we are treading the path of absolute obedience.

It takes misrepresentation to test the consecration of a Christian.

Be thou wholly for God; and He, with all His power, will be wholly for thee.

Nothing that we lose by yielding is worth what we gave.

CONSECRATION (Cont.)

Let God fill up your emptiness and empty your fullness.

"Thy will be done" is the keynote to which every prayer should be tuned.

Whatever is done in God's will can never be a failure.

To let go, is surrender; to let God, is belief.

God will accept a broken heart, but He must have all the pieces.

God cannot have His way while we are in the way. He asks us to let Him put us out of the way.

Where God leads, He will light us.

COURTESY

Gentleness - Politeness

The gentleness of Christ is the comeliest ornament that any Christian can wear.

Nothing costs so little and goes so far as Christian courtesy.

There is no law against being polite, even when you are not a candidate for some office.

Some people should be sentenced to solitary refinement.

The measure of a truly great man is the courtesy with which he treats little men.

You can tell how far up in heaven a man has been by the gentleness and beauty of his social behavior.

COURTESY (Cont.)

No soul can be bathed in the fellowship of divine communion and then descend to earth to play the bore and the bully.

Ecc (03) Nothing is so strong as gentleness; nothing so gentle as real strength.

Courtesy is a duty the servants of Christ owe to the humblest person on earth.

Life is not so short but that there is always time for courtesy.

A gracious word is an easy obligation.

How sweet and gracious even in common speech is that fine sense which men call courtesy!

Courtesy is a science of the highest importance which ought to be on the curriculum of every Christian.

A little of the oil of courtesy will save a lot of friction.

The test of good manners is being able to put up pleasantly with bad ones.

If we must disagree, let us not be disagreeable.

Modern politeness consists of a man offering his seat to a woman when he gets off the bus.

DILIGENCE

Idleness - Industriousness - Laziness

Where one evil spirit tempts the busy man, a thousand tempt the idle man.

It is better for a pot to boil over than never to boil at all.

DILIGENCE (Cont.)

It is better to burn out than to rust out.

An athlete is usually a dignified bunch of muscles unable to split wood or spade dirt.

What a man is depends largely on what he does when he has nothing to do.

The revolving fan gathers no flies. *Ecc (02)*

Too many people itch for what they want but won't scratch for it.

The man with time to burn never gave the world any light.

There is more trouble in having nothing to do than in having much to do.

When inertia gets the better of you, it is time to telephone the undertaker.

People who have nothing to do are usually tired of their own company.

An idle person is the devil's playfellow.

If the devil catches a man idle, he will set him to work.

An idle man never has time.

The industrious man may be tempted of the devil, but the idle man tempts the devil to tempt him.

Between the great things we can't do and the little things we won't do, the danger is we shall do nothing.

Stagnation is the first station this side of perdition.

The devil is never too busy to rock the cradle of a sleeping saint.

God commends us to the ceaseless industry of the ant for noiseless eloquence.

DILIGENCE (Cont.)

When one considers all Christ has done for him, it should cause him to root out every lazy hair in his head.

God doesn't say, "Pray that preachers may go forth into the harvest," but to pray that laborers may go.

Poverty is usually the side-partner of laziness.

Idleness is the burial of a living man, death anticipated.

Standing pools gather the filth.

Idle bodies are generally busybodies.

While ten men wait for something to turn up, one man turns something up.

An idler is a watch that lacks both hands, as useless as when it stands.

The fellow who has an abundance of push gets along without a pull.

The lazier a man is the more he intends to do tomorrow.

Undertake some worthwhile labor that the devil may always find you occupied.

Some fellows are always behind time until it's time to quit.

In the world there are only two ways of raising one's self: by one's own industry or by the weakness of others.

Few things are impossible to diligence.

Plough deep while the sluggards sleep. *Benjamin Franklin.*

DILIGENCE (Cont.)

Bread earned by the sweat of the brow is far sweeter than the tasteless loaf of idleness.

Want of diligence rather than want of means causes most of the failures.

The lazy man aims at nothing and generally hits it.

FAITH

Belief - Trust

Real faith never goes home with an empty basket.

Faith is the soul's intake: love is the soul's outlet.

We believe in a thing when we are prepared to act as if it were true.

The heavenly Father often has to knock out all our props before we will settle down upon Him.

Give us a faith that will not worry, whine, or wrangle but watch, work, wait, and warble.

— Care not whether men say you are a great thinker. *Ecc (03)* See to it that they know you as a great believer.

The beginning of anxiety is the end of faith and the beginning of real faith is the end of anxiety.

You can't get a grain of faith into a disobedient heart.

He who is poor in faith here will be bankrupt hereafter.

He is rich in fact who is rich in faith.

A man may be at his wit's end, but he need not be at his faith's end.

If we desire an increase of faith, we must consent to its testings.

The intuitions of faith are more certain than the conclusions of logic.

It is impossible for faith to overdraw its account in God's bank.

Faith is the key that unlocks the cabinet of promises and empties out their treasures into the soul.

God gives our blessings but we have to take them.

The living God is my Partner. *George Muller.*

Almost without exception, he who has put faith out of his heart has first put obedience out of his life.

Faith itself can go no further than the Word of God but must always be limited by "It is written."

Faith is saying amen to God.

The faith that bears and suffers is greater than the faith that triumphs.

Faith knows that God's bonds are as good as ready money.

A firm faith in the promises of God is the best theology.

To do and suffer God's will is still the highest form of faith, the most sublime Christian achievement.

Great faith is exhibited not so much in ability to do, as to suffer.

It is hard to see how a great man can be an atheist. Doubters do not achieve. Skeptics do not contribute. Cynics do not create. Faith is the great motive power and no man realizes his full possibilities unless he has the deep conviction that life is eternally impor-

FAITH (Cont.)

tant and that his work, well done, is a part of an un-ending plan. *Calvin Coolidge.*

Faith expects from God what is beyond all expectation.

Faith has three elements: knowledge, assent and appropriation.

The devil hasn't armies enough to capture one saint of God who dares to trust Him.

Faith is a higher faculty than reason.

Faith is the link that binds our nothingness to Almightiness.

Faith never comes to a wall too high for it to surmount.

Faith heals only because it brings us into union with His power.

If you want God to honor you, get into the habit of taking Him at His word.

The steps of faith fall on the seeming void and find the Rock beneath. *John Greenleaf Whittier.*

Faith is letting down our nets into the untransparent depths at the divine command, not knowing what we shall take.

Little faith will bring your soul to heaven, but great faith will bring heaven to your soul.

Rest upon His promises though He seem to kill thee.

There is no better way to show our trust in God than to busy ourselves in the things He asks us to do.

When God has a gigantic task to be performed, faith gets the contract.

FAITH (Cont.)

The great believers have ever been the unwearied waiters.

The greatness of our fear shows us the littleness of our faith.

Trust God without terms.

Faith never yet outstripped the bounty of the Lord.

You do not test the resources of God until you try the impossible.

Faith either removes mountains or tunnels through.

Man's greatest strength is often shown in his ability to stand still and trust.

Those who are most diffident of themselves may be most confident in God.

Faith is the heroism of intellect.

Faith lights one through the dark to Deity.

Faith is the subtle chain that binds us to the Infinite.

Faith can stifle all science.

One will never be a hero in anything unless he is first a hero in faith.

None live so pleasantly as those who live by faith.

Faith draws the poison from every grief and takes the sting from every loss.

FAITHFULNESS

Courage - Cowardice - Fidelity - Purpose
Steadfastness

One deserves small credit for being able to start something. The man who can stay with it is the best man.

What you can do, you ought to do; and what you ought to do, by the help of God do.

God has no larger field for the man who is not faithfully doing his work where he is.

Go forward—cost what it may. We have no armor on our backs.

The man who lacks courage to make a start has made a finish already.

When you can't remove an obstacle, plow around it.

The drummer boy who never learned to beat the retreat won a lot of victories.

The tree does not fall at the first stroke.

Any coward can praise Christ, but it takes a man of courage to follow Him.

In trying to get to the top, don't place too much dependence upon the elevator.

Don't give up: success is nothing but failure wearing a fresh coat of paint.

It is human to stand with the crowd. It is divine to stand alone.

Count on God and move forward.

FAITHFULNESS (Cont.)

It is not success that God rewards but always the faithfulness of doing His will.

It is far less important to die the martyr's death than to live the courageous life.

Let the outward condition of God's people be what it may, there is a path of devotedness open to the individual saint, which he can pursue independently of everything.

A good deal of talent is lost in the world for the want of a little courage.

When faithfulness is most difficult, it is most necessary.

Perfect valor is to do without witnesses what one would do before all the world.

One man with courage makes a majority.

The greater danger for most of us is not that our aim is too high and we miss it but that is too low and we reach it.

It often takes more courage to face ridicule than a cannon.

When you get to the end of your rope, tie a knot in it and hang on.

No backbone is stronger than its weakest vertebra.

You can do anything you want, if you want to do what you ought to do.

You can't be down in the mouth and up on your toes at the same time.

Consider the postage stamp: its usefulness lies in its ability to stick to one thing until its gets there.

Constant fidelity in small things is a real and heroic virtue.

FAITHFULNESS (Cont.)

It is courage that vanquishes in war and not good weapons.

There can be no constancy but in an honest cause.

True courage is like a kite; a contrary wind raises it higher.

The root of all steadfastness is in consecration to God.

The one man who is worse than a quitter is the man who is afraid to begin.

The Lord pity the man with a gigantic brain and a tadpole backbone.

Some say that when Eve was made, it was Adam's backbone that was taken instead of his rib.

FORGIVENESS

Thrice blessed is he who can't remember the things he ought to forget about others.

Ecc(ov) Don't bury a mad dog with his tail sticking up above the ground. Forgive and forget.

— It's a lot better to pardon too much than to condemn too much.

We would never have known God had He not said to us, "I will forgive your iniquities."

To err is human; to forgive is divine.

If all were known, all would be forgiven.

— A coward never forgives.

Forgive others often; yourself never.

⁓ Only the brave know how to forgive.

When God pardons, He consigns the offense to everlasting forgetfulness. We are to forgive others as God forgives us.

Those who are ever in need of forgiveness ought to make it their first duty to forgive.

Never does the human soul appear so strong as when it dares to forgive an injury.

We should forgive the penitent for their sake, the impenitent for our own.

It is usually easier to forgive an enemy than a friend.

Ecc(00) No revenge is so complete as forgiveness.

Some forgive their enemies, but not until they are hanged.

Ecc(02) He who cannot forgive others breaks the bridge over which he himself must pass.

— To return evil for good is devilish; to return good for good is human; to return good for evil is Godlike.

He who has not forgiven an enemy has never tasted one of the most sublime enjoyments of life.

It is impudent to ask of God forgiveness on your own behalf, if you refuse to exercise the forgiving temper with respect to others.

Ecc(02) Forgiveness ought to be like a cancelled note, burned up so that it never can be shown against a man.

There is a kind of hedgehog forgiveness, shot out at a person like sharp quills.

Some set the offender before the blowpipe of their indignation, and when they have scorched him enough they forgive him.

FRIENDSHIP

Adversity is the only balance with which to weigh friends.

Ecc(02) He who ceases to be your friend never was a good one.

A friend that you can buy with presents can be bought away from you.

Let friendship creep gently to a height. If it rush, it may run itself out of breath.

A pail that slops over soon empties itself.

He who never made an enemy never made much of a friend.

Promises may get friends, but it is performances that keep them.

Your needy friend may someday be a friend indeed.

Have no friends you dare not bring home.

Friendships cemented together with sin do not hold.

Every man should keep a fair sized cemetery in which to bury the faults of his friends.

The firmest friendships have been formed in mutual adversity, as iron is more strongly united by the fiercest flame.

Friendships are the purer and the more ardent the nearer they come to the presence of God.

If you want to keep your friends, do not give them away.

The best way to wipe out a friendship is to sponge on it.

FRIENDSHIP (Cont.)

Ecc(02)

You'll never have a friend if you must have a friend without a fault.

No friendship can excuse a sin.

Kindred weaknesses induce friendships as often as kindred virtues.

The friendship that is begun for an end will not continue to the end.

If you are a true friend, your heart is like a bell that strikes every time your friend is in trouble.

A friendship that makes the least noise is often the most useful.

It is as much a part of friendship to be delicate in its demands as to be ample in its performances.

False friendship, like the ivy, decays and ruins the walls it embraces.

Some friends remain faithful to us in misfortune, but only the loftiest will reman faithful after our errors and sins have come to light.

Perfect friendship puts us under the necessity of being virtuous.

GENEROSITY

Giving - Covetousness
Stinginess - Tithing - Wealth

When you give someone a cup of milk, don't skim it.

To give in one's lifetime is true generosity; to bequeath after death is mere convenience.

GENEROSITY (Cont.)

If truth takes possesion of a man's heart, it will direct his hand to his pocketbook.

You haven't begun to give until you feel glad over it.

Usually as men's bank accounts increase, their souls shrivel.

When we pray to God for the needs of men, we should also ask Him to consume the selfishness which expends our means upon ourselves.

Some quarrel with their neighbors for the privilege of paying their carfare then select pennies to put in the church collection.

The Lord takes notice, not only of what we give but of what we have left.

When you rob God, you cheat yourself.

The man who dies with a dollar in his pocket is a dollar out.

It may cost something to pay the tithe to the Lord, but it costs a heap more not to pay it.

Christianity is a purse-and-all religion.

You can't take your money to heaven, but you can send it on ahead.

Giving is not just a way of raising money. It is God's way of raising men.

Some people will trust God for the salvation of their souls, but they won't trust Him with the key to their cash boxes.

If there were coins as small as a mill, some people would go to church ten times on a cent.

GENEROSITY (Cont.)

It is easy to be generous with other people's money and to give right and left that which costs us nothing.

When some men give a dollar, they try to convert themselves into a billboard with a megaphone attachment.

The tithe is God's cure for covetousness.

The possessor of a fat pocketbook usually enjoys the distinction of having a lean soul.

You may give without loving, but you cannot love without giving.

The millionaires of eternity are the givers of time.

The liberal man is the man whose riches are likely to continue with him.

Some men are benevolent; others are beneficent. One is well-wishing; the other is well-doing.

Take heed, lest by growing rich you grow worth nothing at last.

Selfishness with much can do little, but love with little can do much.

Giving should be based on principle, regulated by system, beautified by self-sacrifice.

Avarice gathers itself poor; charity pays itself rich.

Of great riches there is no use except in the distribution.

The philanthropist is often one who returns to the people publicly a small amount of what he steals from them privately.

The folks who never give away any milk until after they skim it are sure to want credit for cream.

GENEROSITY (Cont.)

It is the things we cannot spare which make our offerings alive.

A man does not own his wealth; he owes it.

Giving advice to the poor is about as near charity as some people ever get.

He who honors the Lord will give Him his substance as well as his sentiment.

Some men pray high but give low.

When the heart in converted, the purse will be inverted.

Some who are generous with other people's money are famous for refusing themselves nothing.

Don't try to cheat the Lord and call it economy.

Pretending to be rich keeps many people poor.

Love of the right use of money is the root of much good.

Give not from the top of your purse but from the bottom of your heart.

Unconsecrated wealth of Christians is one of the greatest hindrances to the church's progress.

Wanting less is sometimes greater riches than having more.

None but the crazy give alms to the lazy.

It is not what we take up but what we give up that makes us rich.

God looks not to the quantity of the gift but to the quality of the giver.

Great abundance of riches cannot by any means be both gathered and kept without sin.

GENEROSITY (Cont.)

When a man begins to amass wealth, it is a question whether God is going to gain a fortune or lose a man.

Real consecration is sure to regulate the use of one's money.

The longest chapter in the Bible (Numbers 7, nearly 2,000 words) is about giving.

Some say, "Give till it hurts," but it hurts some people to give a nickel.

Many a poor man is as much caught in the toils of the love of money as the rich.

He who keeps close to God will not be close with God.

Philanthropic unbelievers and unphilanthropic believers are equally monstrosities.

Stinginess is that detestable vice which no one will forgive in others, and few are without themselves.

HEAVEN

Heaven's gates are wide enough to admit sinners saved by grace, but too narrow to admit any sin.

The love of heaven makes one heavenly.

Nothing is farther than earth from heaven: nothing is nearer than heaven to earth.

The joy of heaven begins as soon as we attain the character of heaven.

He who seldom thinks of heaven is not likely to get there.

He who is on the road to heaven will not be content to go there alone.

It is impossible to have a real hope of heaven and be deeply engrossed in the pleasures of earth.

If the way to heaven is narrow, it is not long; and if the gate be straight, it opens into endless life.

Heaven is the day of which grace is the dawn—the ripe fruit of which grace is the lovely flower.

God's spiritual temple contains vessels of various dimensions, but all are filled with the same Spirit from the communicable fullness of Christ.

There will be degrees in glory, but all shall be full of joy.

A man may lose the good things of this life against his will; but if he loses the joys of heaven, he does so with his own consent.

Love heaven and you cannot miss it. The love of Christ takes heaven by storm.

Where Jesus is—'tis heaven there.

A true saint every day takes a turn in heaven. His thoughts and desires are like birds flying up to paradise.

As the needle trembles until it stands at the north, so the soul, once united to Christ, cannot be at rest until it arrives at the heavenly home.

A vision of the heavenly Jerusalem must inspire within one a vehement heavenliness.

Separation is the law of earth, but there are no distances in heaven.

To have Jesus ever with us will be the acme and sum of all happiness, of all perfection, of all good.

Jesus is the joy and glory of heaven. We love heaven only as we love Him.

One tear, one sight, one fear, one loss, one thought of trouble, cannot find lodging there.

It is impossible to conceive of man in a high and happy state without an employment worthy of that estate, constituting its dignity and happiness.

To read some descriptions of heaven, one would imagine it were only an endless prolongation of some social meeting.

Eternity makes heaven to be heaven. Oh blessed day that shall have no night!

Heaven is a state where we will be growing happier and happier as ages pass away, yet leaving nothing still happier to come.

No night there! Night is associated with the idea of weariness and is the symbol of ignorance, sin, danger, want, and death.

You will not see heaven the first day you get there. You cannot see Rome in six weeks. It will take all eternity to examine the trophies of the New Jerusalem.

"They rest not day nor night." To hush their music and stop their action would be to heaven's inhabitants intolerable toil.

If it were possible to enter heaven void of holiness, it would be no place of happiness.

A sinful heart must have sinful delights and sinful company. Heaven would be as hell to an unregenerate soul.

Count upon it: no one will enter heaven who is a rebel, steeped in the guilt of rebellion against Christ.

If a sinner without Christ could creep into heaven, he would carry within him hell fire that would give him no rest.

Heaven must be begun below in all those who shall enjoy its perfections above.

None but the holy can look upon the holy One.

Heaven would be hell to an irreligious man. One who cannot stand a prayer meeting here would find no satisfaction there.

Heaven itself would be fire to those who would vain escape across the great gulf from the torments of hell.

The law of variety which shines in the earthly exhibition of Christianity will shed its fascinations over paradise and lend its zest to the services of heaven.

What delight it will afford to renew the sweet counsel we have had on earth, to recount the toils of combat and the labor of the way!

Heaven is called "my Father's house"—and shall not His housemates be known to each other?

As with two luminous bodies, each may shine in perfection, though with different splendor and intensity, so the image of God will shine with fuller orbed splendor in some than in others.

The spirits of the just made perfect shall all be beautiful, but some shall delight with the perfection of beauty.

HELL

Future Retribution

Hell is prepared only for those who prepare it for themselves by kindling its fires here and now.

Hell is God's very best for those who reject His Son.

Hell is full of good meanings and wishes.

Christianity knocks man out of hell and hell out of man.

Where is hell? At the end of an ungodly life.

The man who is interested in proving there is no hell generally has a personal reason for doing so.

Hell's mouth is open wide enough without making it any wider by preaching second chance.

Every soul-winner believes in hell.

A true fear of hell has sent many a soul to heaven.

No man ever seeks heaven very anxiously until he believes in a hell.

There are some wonderful parking places on the road to hell.

Souls stumble into hell over two persons: the moral outsider and the immoral insider.

War is worse than the modern ideas of hell.

Hell is truth seen too late.

Hell is paved with good intentions.

Many might go to heaven with half the labor with which they go to hell.

HELL (Cont.)

Hell is knowing that every chance of excellence and every opportunity of good has been lost forever.

Hell is the common pit into which all the streams of sin and misery disgorge themselves as rivers do their streams into the vast ocean.

Grant that hell fire is but a symbol of the punishment which awaits the unbelieving: in what respects have they who have persuaded themselves of this, improved their prospects?

As sure as night follows day and winter follows summer, so shall wrath follow sin.

HOME

When home is ruled by Christ, angels might be asked to stay all night and would not find themselves out of their element.

No man can safely go abroad who does not love to stay at home.

Many modern homes are merely filling stations.

Home is a place where we are treated best and grumble most.

Many a man who is a big bug at the office is just an insect at home.

Home is the chief school of human virtues.

Home should interpret heaven and should be heaven for beginners.

Home is the sweetest type of heaven.

King or peasant, he is happiest who finds peace at home.

HOME (Cont.)

The first indication of domestic happiness is the love of one's home.

The homes of a nation are the bulwark of personal and national safety.

Home is never perfectly furnished for enjoyment unless there is a little child rising up in it.

Let your home face toward the Father's house.

A house is no home unless it contains food for the soul as well as for the body.

Home should be the ground floor of heaven; departure from this life, just going up stairs.

A little girl, asked where her home was, replied, "Where Mother is."

A man's home should be on the hilltop of cheerfulness, so high that no shadows might rest upon it.

In this wintry world, it is a tender mother's love and a pious mother's care that are the carpet on the floor and the blaze on the evening hearth of home.

To Adam, paradise was home; and to the good among his descendants, home is paradise.

HONESTY

Cheating - Dishonesty - Integrity

Some people worry so much about St. Peter's ledger that they forget all about their account on the grocer's ledger.

The white man who begins by cheating a black ends up by cheating a white man.

HONESTY (Cont.)

If some men wore only what clothes really belong to them, they would have on nothing but a necktie and a pair of socks.

People who are very prompt at paying grudges are often very slow in paying their bills.

It is hard to pay for bread that has been eaten.

Every enemy you make by doing the square thing is a rascal at heart.

No man is liable to give his fellowmen a square deal until he first has given God a square deal.

Honesty is the best policy, especially when you may want to borrow something on your policy.

Some men are known by their deeds, others by their mortgages.

Only by being on the level can men climb to the highest place.

Buy not silk while you owe for milk.

Father's fraud drives his sons abroad.

The badge of honesty is simplicity.

A rich man ought to be an honest man, for he would be a double knave to cheat men when he had no need of it.

The sun has no need to boast of its brightness, and honest people have little to say about their honesty.

Nothing so completely baffles one who is full of duplicity himself as straightforward and simple integrity in another.

However difficult it may be for integrity to get on, it is a thousand times more difficult for knavery to get off.

HONESTY (Cont.)

Though a hundred crooked paths may lead to temporary success, the one plain path of honesty alone can lead to lasting fame and the blesings of posterity.

HUMILITY

Meekness

Exalt yourself and you'll not come nigh Him. Humble yourself and He will descend to you.

The greatness of lowliness to which we are called is His own greatness: He came not to be ministered unto but to minister.

To be good should be more our care than to have preeminence.

The great man is the man who does not lose his child's heart.

When we grow away from childlikeness, we are in a decline.

Few people have a lower opinion of themselves than they deserve.

The flowers of Christian graces grow only under the shade of the cross, and the root of them all is humility.

Humility is a virtue all preach, some practice, and everybody is content to hear praised.

God demands a whole heart, but He accepts a broken one.

True humility is the emptiness of self which God fills.

HUMILITY (Cont.)

Humility is the acceptance of the place appointed by God, whether it is in the front or in the rear.

— A good violinist is one with ability to play first fiddle and a willingness to play second.

He never rises high who does not know how to kneel.

He is truly a humble man who does not feel proud when people praise him for his humility.

The young Christian thinks himself little. The growing Christian thinks he is nothing. The mature Christian knows he is less than nothing.

Humbleness is always dignity.

Do not practice excessive humility.

The doctrine of grace humbles man without degrading him and exalts him without inflating him.

The grace that makes every grace amiable is humility.

No man will learn anything at all unless he will first learn humility.

The beloved of the Almighty are the rich who have the humility of the poor and the poor who have the magnanimity of the rich.

He who places himself neither higher nor lower than he ought to, exercises the truest humility.

Do you wish to be great? Begin by being little. Think first about the foundations of humility.

Get in the place of humility, and you will be in the place of power.

The man who bows the lowest in the presence of God stands the straightest in the presence of sin.

HUMILITY (Cont.)

Whom God would greatly exalt He first humbles.

Only when the heart is a broken vessel can it carry the water of life.

Those who know God will be humble. Those who know themselves cannot be proud.

All who would reach the Mount of Transfiguration must go by the way of the Valley of Humiliation.

The great man is the man who is little enough to let God be great.

He who blushes at the discovery of his own hidden virtues is a true gentleman.

The branches that bear the most fruit hang the lowest.

The higher a man gets in divine grace the lower he will be in his own esteem.

It is not a sign of humility to declaim against pride.

The humblest occupation has in it discipline which fits one for the highest heaven.

The only way up is down.

The Lord uses those who see themselves little in their own eyes.

God has two thrones: one in the highest heaven and the other in the lowliest heart.

The holiest saint is ever getting lower.

The work an unknown man does is like a vein of water flowing hidden under ground, secretly making the ground green.

Eliot The Christian is humble because he has given up seeking good in himself to adore the One in whom there is nothing but good.

64

HUMILITY (Cont.)

Great men are the ones unconscious of greatness; only little men must increase their size by inflation.

Meekness is not weakness but strength harnessed for service.

If you think God's thoughts, you'll never think highly of yourself.

We can't have the lowly life unless we have the upper life.

The smaller we are, the more room God has.

To sink is the way to rise; to serve is the way to rule.

The world's greatness is measured by authority and lordliness, but divine greatness is a meek and gentle influence.

HYPOCRISY

Formalism - Inconsistency

To formalists a breach of external piety is far more shocking than a breach of principle.

Men say they are not themselves when tempted by evil to betray what they really are.

Piety used as a pull soon gets frayed out.

Religion is the best armor a man can have, but the worst cloak.

It is the inconsistent Christian who helps the devil most.

A mote in the gunner's eyes is as bad as a spike in the gun.

HYPOCRISY (Cont.)

There's nothing that locks the lips of a Christian like an inner life that is not right.

Some people have too much religion to be happy at a dance, but too little to be happy at a prayer meeting.

If you are going to hell, don't go by way of the communion table.

A fair skin often covers a crooked mind.

The fellow who is six days worldly and one day pious is, in fact, seven days worldly and not pious at all.

Some men haven't any opinions but yours, until they meet the next fellow.

A man's character is like a fence: all the white-wash in the world won't strengthen it.

God would as soon see people in their nakedness and being what they actually are, as trying to cloak their hypocrisy. Be what you are.

God can't be cheated with deftly quoted texts. He looks on the heart.

Religion is a cloak used by some in this world who will not feel the need of a cloak in the next world.

Many professing Christians sing, "I'm a child of the King," but they live impoverished lives.

To be a Christian and have no one suspect it is an impossibility.

Eccl(ou) The world does not doubt Christianity as much as it does some Christians.

We have no right to sing, "In the cross of Christ I glory," unless we are willing to add, "By whom the world is crucified unto me and I unto the world."

66

HYPOCRISY (Cont.)

Some people devote all their religion to going to church.

Some people pray and talk cream but live skimmed milk.

Many will give Christianity their countenance but will not give it their heart.

The religion of Christ is either the chief concern of the soul, or it is a fraud and a mockery.

The hypocrite steals the uniform of the court of heaven to serve the devil in.

God has no enemy, and Satan no tool like the zealous professor of Christianity whose life is not directed and sustained by the indwelling Spirit of God.

Many call the church their mother whom God will not own as His children.

One repulsive Christian will drive away a score of prodigals.

Much weeping in a meeting is not a sure evidence of much piety. A fountain pen leaks when it is nearest empty.

Heathen are true to false gods, while professed Christians are often false to the true God.

Hypocritical piety is double iniquity.

Some talk Christianity by the yard, but they cannot live it by the inch.

Knock down a hypocrite in the church, and you'll upset a dozen outsiders who are leaning against him.

A week filled up with selfishness and a Sunday full of religious exercises will make a good pharisee but a poor Christian.

HYPOCRISY (Cont.)

Many lustily sing, "Crown Him Lord of all" who do not recognize His rights on a single foot of the soil of their inheritance.

The gospel professed may lift a man up to heaven, but only the gospel possessed will get him into heaven.

Where deeds pull down, words can repair no faith.

The devil is surpassingly cunning; and, if he can, he will mix an opiate even with the communion wine.

Periodical godliness is perpetual hypocrisy.

Hypocrites are the greatest dupes the devil has. They serve him better than any other but receive no wages.

Some people have heaven on their tongues, but the world is on their fingers' ends.

It is common for those who have estranged themselves from the vitals of religion to discover a great fondness for the externals of it.

The effort to express more than we feel eventually destroys what feeling we have.

The darkest shadows of life are those which a man makes when he stands in his own light.

Do not curse the devil openly and bless him secretly.

A grease spot on a man's suit of clothes is what you will remember of the way he was dressed, and we remember men by the spots on their characters.

Better be one-sided than two-faced.

There is no greater mistake than to suppose that Christians can impress the world by compromising with it.

HYPOCRISY (Cont.)

It is in many places a lost labor to seek for Christianity among Christians.

INFLUENCE

Example

Others will follow your footsteps easier than they will follow your advice.

It is easier to adopt the weaknesses of a friend than his good qualities.

A Christian may be a blot or a blessing; a blank he cannot be.

A Christian is a living sermon whether or not he preaches a word.

A Christian's life is the world's Bible.

One example is worth a thousand arguments.

A pint of example is worth a gallon of advice.

You cannot lift others to a higher level than that on which you live yourself.

There is not one inconsistent Christian but does unaccountable mischief.

Next to the might of the Spirit of God, the silent beauty of a holy life is the most powerful influence in the world.

Every man is a missionary, whether or not he intends it or designs it.

There is not a soul who does not either increase or diminish the sum total of human happiness.

Example is more forcible than precept.

INFLUENCE (Cont.)

Examples hasten deeds to good effects.

A consistent life is the best interpreter and proof of the gospel.

No reproof is so potent as the silent influence of a good example.

We are less convinced by what we hear than by what we see.

None preaches better than the ant, and she says nothing.

The strongest argument that can be offered a skeptic is a godly life.

We reform others unconsciously when we walk uprightly.

There are preachers who preach so well it is a shame they must ever leave the pulpit and who live so poorly it is a shame they should ever go into the pulpit.

Men trust rather to their eyes than to their ears.

A minister's practice is as much if not more regarded than his preaching.

Precept is instruction written in the sand. The tide flows over it and the record is gone. Example is graven on the rock.

Nothing does more to enlarge the gulf of atheism than the want of conformity between the profession and the practice of Christians.

Never was there good or ill done that did not produce its like.

Corkscrews have sunk more people than cork jackets ever saved.

INFLUENCE (Cont.)

Some men let 1000 gallons of beer drain through them in order to get the value of 1¾ pounds of beefsteak.

INTEMPERANCE

Temperance

The best temperance lecture is to see a fellow hunting a job with booze on his breath.

Two things make unhappy homes: men's love for wet goods and women's love for dry goods.

Alcohol kills the living and preserves the dead.

Plain living and high thinking go together.

Temperateness is the nurse of chastity.

Many a man has dug his grave with his teeth.

Suppers have slain as many as the sword.

Dieting is the triumph of mind over platter.

Dignity is one thing that can't be preserved in alcohol.

Even from the standpoint of a man's temporal interests, a man should be wise enough to leave liquor alone.

One who cannot resist the temptation to food will easily be mastered by the sparkling cup.

Other vices make their own way, but the vice of intemperance makes way for all vices.

He that is a drunkard is qualified for all vice.

Intemperance is voluntary madness.

INTEMPERANCE (Cont.)

Liquor displays every little spot of the soul in its utmost deformity.

Drinking pure water never made a man sick nor in debt, nor his wife a widow.

Temperance is a virtue which casts the truest luster upon the person in which it lodges.

KNOWLEDGE
Education - Fools - Learning - Wisdom

Some read just enough to keep themselves misinformed.

Many have gained a reputation for wisdom by imitating the owl.

The doorstep to the temple of wisdom is a knowledge of your own ignorance.

Some men go to college to learn to express their ignorance in scientific terms.

Knowledge humbles the great man, astonishes the common man, and puffs up the little man.

No sense is so uncommon as common sense.

There is no worse error than to seek an intellectual remedy for a moral grief.

Knowledge is proud that he has learned so much; Wisdom is humble that he knows no more.

Christianity makes one educated, cultured, and moral; but these things do not make a Christian.

There are forty men of wit to one of sense.

He who will not learn of anyone except himself has a fool for a teacher.

Consciousness of ignorance is no small part of knowledge.

A professor is a man whose job it is to tell students how to solve the problems of life which he himself has tried to avoid by becoming a professor.

The only way to receive the mind of Christ is to lose your own.

Wise is the man who knows enough not to know too much.

The wisest man is the man who has made up his mind to be "a fool for Christ's sake."

Education cannot cure sin: it only sharpens sin's tools.

Every truth we know is a candle given us to work by. All knowledge is lost which ends in the knowing.

The thing that surprises the college man most when he gets out into the world is to find out how much uneducated people know that he doesn't.

Education is the development of power, not an accumulation of facts.

Many a man counted a fool by financiers has laid up in heaven a fortune they would envy.

Without actual work to do, the head is just a loafing place for thoughts and ideas.

It is not honking your horn that keeps you out of trouble as much as steering wisely.

Knowledge is power only under three conditions: if it is knowledge of things worth knowing; if it is known by a person worthy of using it; and if it be used.

It is better to know less than to know a lot that isn't so.

He who is not aware of his ignorance, will only be misled by his knowledge.

A wise man is like a pin: his head keeps him from going too far.

It takes diplomacy to get a diploma.

A college education never hurt anyone who was willing to learn something afterward.

A brain is as strong as its weakest think.

The worst thing about wisdom is that it can only be acquired on the installment plan.

The head begins to swell when the mind stops growing.

That man is sure to go wrong in his thinking whose aim is to get for himself.

The man who can't think is not an educated man, no matter how many college degrees he may have acquired.

There isn't any objection to a college training, except that it postpones some fellows' education for four years.

There is as much horse sense as ever, but it is mostly horses that have it.

It is difficult to say a sensible thing nowadays. *Abraham Lincoln.*

Hell hath no fury like a zealot trying to prove a theory.

Merely having an open mind is nothing. The object of opening the mind, as of opening the mouth, is to shut it again on something solid.

Knowledge is folly unless grace guide it.

Half-knowledge is worse than ignorance.

Knowledge advances by steps, not by leaps.

If you have worthwhile knowledge, let others light their candles at it.

The wisest among us is a fool in some things.

True wisdom is seldom gained without suffering.

He who is not too wise is wise.

As for me, all I know is that I know nothing. *Socrates.*

No man can be wise on an empty stomach.

The wisest man is generally he who thinks himself least so.

It is good to rub and polish your brain against that of others.

A wise man will always be a Christian because the perfection of wisdom is to know where lies tranquility of mind.

He who considers himself a paragon of wisdom is sure to commit some superlatively stupid act.

Some men are born fools, but the majority become so from practice.

What a pity human beings can't exchange problems. Everyone knows exactly how to solve the other fellow's.

LOVE

Forbearance - Kindness - Mercy - Patience

Religion that fails to mellow the heart, making more tender and kind, patient and forbearing with others, is not that of Christ .

We can't be blind to other people's faults; but we can be infinitely tender, comparing their worst with our worst and not their worst with our best.

It is beautiful to see an injured, disappointed man protective and kindly to others.

Nature says love thyself. Domestic education says love your family. Patriotism says love your country. Christianity says love all mankind.

Love is the diamond among the jewels of the believer's breastplate.

Kindness to the needy is but a flower of Eden that still clings to the ruins of our nature.

If slighted, slight the slight and love the slighter.

Kind words take less breath than harsh ones.

The tombstone way is the best way: it always sticks up for one when he is down.

Some men, by hating vice too much, come to love men too little.

Unless you lovingly bear with the fault of a friend, you betray your own.

God's love will leak out of our hearts if we are not watchful unto prayer.

A little of the oil of Christlike love will save a lot of friction.

LOVE (Cont.)

Guard within yourself that treasure, kindness. Know how to give without hesitation, lose without regret, acquire without meanness.

The help that is given as a matter of duty without the love of the heart will be worth little and soon will cease to flow .

If love to God does not find a field for its manifestation in active love to man, worship in the temple will be mockery.

He is not truly patient who is willing to suffer only so much as he thinks good and from whom he pleases.

There is nothing like a grace-filled disposition for putting the devil to flight.

Don't wait until a man puts on his wooden overcoat before you speak the word of kindness to him.

Duty makes us do things well, but love makes us do them beautifully.

We can measure our likeness to the Saviour by the range of our sensitiveness to the world's sorrow and pain.

A more glorious victory over another cannot be gained than to meet with kindness the injury that began on the other's part.

Some men preserve their orthodoxy in vinegar.

When one man differs from another, there is opportunity for growth in love and patience.

Kind words are the music of the world.

Loving-kindness has converted more sinners than either zeal, eloquence, or learning.

Every effort made for the happiness of others lifts us above ourselves.

LOVE (Cont.)

Most Christians have not begun to use kind words in such abundance as they ought to be used.

It is easy finding reasons why other folks should be patient and kind.

There is no God-like doing that is not patient doing.

He loves not Christ at all who does not love Christ above all.

As there is no sin without the love of ourselves, so there is no good work without the love of God.

LYING

Deceit - Falsehood

A white lie soon gets tanned from exposure.

Trying to undo a false story after it has started is like trying to gather up a basket of thistle seed after it is scattered.

Sin has many tools, but a lie is a handle that fits them all.

When a lawyer dies, he lies still.

Stretch the truth, and it will fly back and sting you.

Nine tenths of all the lying that people do is to get out of something they've done that's wrong.

All printed lies are black lies.

A whispered lie is just as wrong as one that is thundered loud and long.

A lie begets a lie until they come to generations.

78

LYING (Cont.)

It is easy to tell one lie, but hard to tell just one.

A lie is offered as an asset, but invariably it proves to be a liability.

Lying appears more repulsive when we consider who began it. (*See* John 8:44.)

Those who are given to white lies soon become color blind.

A lie is like a dog chasing its tail. Let it alone and it will chase itself out of breath.

A liar is a man who has no partition between his imagination and his information.

A good thing about telling the truth is that you don't have to remember what you said.

The best way to avoid lying is to do nothing in your relationship with another that needs concealment.

Some people stretch the truth; others mutilate it.

A lie is like a banana peel a man throws on the walk: you're liable to slip up on it yourself later.

Liars are verbal forgers.

A good memory is needed, once you have lied.

It isn't right to lie even about the devil.

None but cowards resort to lies.

A lie that is half a truth is not less a lie than others.

A lie has no legs and cannot stand, but it has wings and can fly far and wide.

The most mischievous liars are those who keep sliding on the verge of truth.

LYING (Cont.)

No man has a good enough memory to be a successful liar. *Abraham Lincoln.*

MARRIAGE

Matrimony

After man came woman, and she has been after him ever since.

Some men marry for beauty; others for booty.

When a husband is fire and the wife is tinder, the devil easily starts a conflagration.

Honeymoons are apt to set like the other moon.

Choose a wife rather by your ear than by your eye.

Judge a maiden at the kneading board, not at the dance.

It is a sorry house in which the hen crows and the cock is silent.

Single women say they wouldn't marry the best man in the world. Married women know they didn't.

Some say singleness is bliss and marriage is a blister.

Love is like the measles—worse if it comes late in life.

The sea of matrimony is filled with hardships.

The fellow who thinks love is only a lottery, usually proves it by drawing a blank.

It takes two to make a marriage—a single girl and an anxious mother.

MARRIAGE (Cont.)

Wedlock should be a padlock.

A bad husband cannot be a good man.

An obedient wife commands her husband.

In marriage two are made one, but the question is, Which one?

In paradise before the fall, God instituted marriage and Jesus first wrought miracles to bless a wedding feast.

Adam laid down and slept, and from his side a woman in her magic beauty rose. Dazzled and charmed, he called that woman bride—and his first sleep became his last repose.

Never be yoked to one who refuses the yoke of Christ.

Plenty of music will keep the husband at home, provided it isn't chin music.

The way to fight a woman is with your hat—grab it and run.

A good wife is like the ivy which beautifies the building to which it clings, twining its tendrils more lovingly as time converts the ancient edifice into a ruin.

Disagreements concealed are half reconciled. A good husband never publicly reproves his wife.

A married man falling into misfortune is more apt to retrieve his situation in the world than a single one.

She that hath a wise husband must entice him to an eternal dearness by the veil of modesty and the robes of chastity.

Never speak loudly to one another unless the house is on fire.

MARRIAGE (Cont.)

Success in marriage is more than *finding* the right person: it is a matter of *being* the right person.

It's a happy home where the wife makes allowance for the husband's shortcomings and the husband makes allowance for the wife's outgoings.

Make this agreement with your wife: if she will quit driving from the back seat, you will quit cooking from the dining room table.

What passes for woman's intuition is often nothing more than man's transparency.

Divorce is the hash made from domestic scraps.

A bachelor is usually a man who has cheated some woman out of a divorce.

The average man lays down the law and then accepts his wife's amendments.

A man always chases a woman until she catches him.

There are two sides to every question: her side and the wrong side.

Some men are born meek and others get married.

Many a man in love with a dimple has made the mistake of marrying the whole girl.

The old-fashioned woman who darned her husband's socks has a daughter who socks her darned husband.

Marriage used to be a contract; now many regard it as a ninety-day option.

When a girl marries a man to mend his ways, she is apt to find that he isn't worth a darn.

Love at first sight never happens before breakfast.

MARRIAGE (Cont.)

Some men rule the house with a rod of irony.

Meet the woman who called her husband theory (not dearie) because he seldom worked.

Marriage is the bloom or blight of happiness.

Hearts with equal love combined kindle never-dying fires.

Marry in haste; repent at leisure.

Keep you eyes wide open before marriage and half shut afterward.

Frequently those who marry where they do not love, love where they do not marry.

MEDITATION

Bible Study - Study

Apply thyself wholly to the Scriptures and the Scriptures wholly to thyself.

When the Word of God is as sweet as honey, the vanities of time are as bitter as aloes.

He who teaches the Word of God is never a scholar: he is always a student.

If you find more pleasure in reading the Sunday newspaper than your Bible, there is something wrong in the heart.

The Bible grows by being read.

The Bible won't be a dry Book if you know its Author.

Bible verses will save you from spiritual reverses.

MEDITATION (Cont.)

Obedience is one of the best commentaries on the Bible. Do what the Bible says, and you'll know it is true.

Satan loves to keep Christians so over busy in "the Lord's work" that the Lord can get no opportunity to tell them what He wants them to do.

Thoughts given out are the most possessed.

The features of Christ are best developed on the tablets of the soul in the darkroom of meditation.

A loving trust in the Author of the Bible is the best preparation for a wise study of the Bible.

It is an awful responsibility to own a Bible.

Many people wonder why they can't understand the Bible when they are reading with wooden spectacles on.

Every truth we know is a candle given us to work by.

A lot of Christians are living on crackers and cheese when God has prepared for them three square meals a day.

Have your tools ready, and God will find you work.

There are multitudes whose Bibles are read only on the edges.

Get the fullness of the Spirit, and you will get deeper views of the Bible.

He who loves the Word will receive the power to understand what he loves.

Use the Word, and it becomes a sword against the devil. Peruse the Word, and it becomes bread unto your own soul.

MEDITATION (Cont.)

The Christian is he who can truly say, "Thy Word have I hid in my heart."

The Bible throws great light upon the commentaries.

— The Bible was not written so much to tell how the heavens go as to tell how to go to heaven.

A desire to have the Scriptures on our side is one thing, and a desire to be on the side of the Scripture is another.

Above all, learn to acquiesce in the truth as soon as it is discovered.

The hidden things of God are not revealed until we are treading the path of obedience.

He who sits at the feet of the Lord and hears His Word is sitting at the feet of the supreme intellect of the world.

Bolted food never unlocks its essences. Meditation is mental mastication.

Tarry at a promise till God meets you there.

Every command of God has a promise of God for its kernel.

The Bible should be read as a religious privilege, not as an act of penance.

As you become less spiritual, your Bible will become less interesting.

The minds of some Bible students are like concrete—thoroughly mixed and permanently set.

He who holds false doctrine holds it first in his own thinking and then seeks it in the Bible as a second source.

MEDITATION (Cont.)

A Bible stored in the mind is worth a dozen stored in the bottom of one's trunk.

To own a Bible and feed on the newspaper is one way to be a lean and dyspeptic Christian.

Every fact of the Bible is meant to be a factor in the life.

Meditation is the soul's perspective glass.

Not he that reads most but he that meditates most on divine truth proves the wisest, choicest Christian.

The more we study, the more we discover our ignorance.

MISSIONS

Evangelization

If a man love not the immigrant in his own country, whom he has seen, how shall he love the foreigner in the heathen country, whom he has not seen?

To say that all Christians are missionaries is the same thing as saying all Christians are Christian. The former must be true if the latter is.

The majority of Christians do not give a penny, a prayer, or a thought in a year to the advancement of Christ's cause in the world.

The church as a whole gives less for the evangelization of the world than is expended in idolatrous worship at a single heathen shrine in India in a year.

We treat Christ the way we treat the heathen.

MISSIONS (Cont.)

Our prayers for the evangelization of the world are but bitter irony so long as we give only our superfluity and then draw back before the sacrifice of ourselves.

It is impossible to bring the world to Jesus, but we can take Jesus to the whole world.

There is a mighty *go* in the word *gospel.*

Every impulse and stroke of missonary power on earth is from the heart of Christ.

Your love has a broken wing if it cannot fly across the sea.

We are saved because of past missionary efforts. What of the coming generation?

You will never win the world for Christ with your spare cash.

God had an only Son, and He was a missionary and physician.

If God wants you on the mission field, neither your money nor your prayers will ever prove an acceptable substitute.

The closer you come to God's altar the more likely you are to be a missionary.

The church that persists in shelving the missionary question is pronouncing its own doom.

If there were more abiding in Christ, there would be fewer Christians abiding in America.

Indifference to missions means the forfeiture of Christ's favor and presence.

Have you the Master's permission to stay home?

MISSIONS (Cont.)

Christ says, "Go ye into all the world," but of every 100,000 communicants in America only 21 go.

At every breath we draw, four souls perish, never having heard of Christ.

God is the Head of the missionary movement. The devil is the advance leader of the opposition.

The one calling not overcrowded is the missionary's.

There is no *home* or *foreign* in God's missionary vocabulary.

People who don't believe in missions should turn back the pages of history and read of the life lived by their ancestors before missionaries reached them.

Charity begins at home, but the kind we read about in the Bible is never confined there.

The largest realization of the presence of Christ is in the widest fulfillment of His command "Go ye."

By what right do you choose your King's last command, "Go ye," as the one thing to be crowded out of your life?

If I refuse to give anything to missions, I cast my ballot in favor of the recall of every missionary.

If the evangelization of this world were a commercial proposition with a reward of even a 10-percent dividend, there would not be a village on earth without a church.

A prayer-laden copper cent given for missions as the result of self-denial outweighs a ten-dollar bill easily and carelessly given.

OPPORTUNITY

Responsibility

God holds us responsible—not for what we have, but could have; not for what we are, but might be.

Many a Christian is not at home when opportunity knocks at his door.

It isn't enough to know an opportunity when you see it. You must be prepared to grasp it and make it yours.

Opportunity often reveals great men in small places and small men in great places.

The most solemn thing in the world is our accountability to God.

There are people who would do great acts; but because they wait for great opportunities, life passes and the acts of love are not done at all.

The doors of opportunity are marked Push.

If God writes *Opportunity* on one side of open doors, He writes *Responsibility* on the other.

Our responsibility never can cease so long as we have a life to live for Christ and a whole world still waiting for the gospel.

God's best gifts to us are not things but opportunities.

We are responsible up to the last particle of our power.

You may recover much that is lost but never a lost opportunity.

Great souls prove their greatness by making opportunities where others only make complaint.

OPPORTUNITY (Cont.)

In the morning, praise God for opportunity; but make some use of it before the morning goes.

The hour of opportunity lies near the hours of prayer.

Opportunity is no respecter of office hours; always be on the job.

Great opportunities come to those who make the most of small ones.

A wise man will make more opportunities than he finds.

Not only strike the iron while it is hot, but keep it hot by striking.

The way to miss success is to miss the opportunity.

The great man is the man who turns to account all opportunities.

Responsibility walks hand in hand with capacity and power.

PEACE

One of the devil's snares is to occupy us with the past and future so as to take away our peace for the present.

If you want to be miserable, look within; distracted, look around; peaceful, look up.

Go where you will—your soul will find no peace but on the bosom of Christ.

Peace rules the day when Christ rules the mind.

Peace won by compromise is a short-lived achievement.

PEACE (Cont.)

Even peace may be purchased at too high a price.

Blessedness is promised to the peacemaker, not the conqueror.

The peace of the soul consists in absolute resignation to the will of Christ.

The peace of Christ rejoices in the midst of adversity and overcomes the cross.

The peace of the saints is meat of which those without know nothing.

There can be no peace where pride reigns.

Set the Lord Jesus betwixt God and your sins, and the work of His righteousness will be your peace.

Peace cannot be bought with all the world's riches nor given by the greatest mortal prince.

None who have tasted of the ravishing delights of divine peace will part with it for the pleasures of sin.

The messengers of Christ went forth with the word *peace* upon their lips, the gift of peace in their hands and the light of peace upon their faces.

The secret of peace is the constant reference of all to the care of God.

If we allow our worries, anxieties, and careworn questionings to brood in our hearts, they will soon break up our peace as tiny gnats will make a paradise uninhabitable.

PRAISE TO GOD

Gratitude - Thanksgiving

Put your thanksgiving into the present tense. It's a sure cure for grumbling.

Give thanks part of the time and live thanks the rest of the time.

Hem your blessings with praise lest they unravel.

The devil fears a thankful Christian.

No Christian has so little from Christ that there is no ground for praise, nor so much that he has no need of prayer.

When you find it hard to pray, begin to give thanks and you'll have an ocean to swim in.

Praise is the blossom of prayer.

Petition goes into God's presence to bring something away, but praise goes into His presence never to return.

Our song of praise can never be checked, unless we rejoice in circumstances and things of earth more than in God Himself.

Mere lip praise is never outlet enough for grateful hearts when God gives ability for other service also.

God loveth a cheerful giver, whether it be the gold of his purse or the gold of his lips which he presents upon His altar.

When prayer is answered, forget not praise. The apparently conquered enemy steals in again at the door of an ungrateful heart.

There are multitudes who cry, "God be merciful" and never say, "God be praised!"

92

PRAISE TO GOD (Cont.)

Never achieve a success without giving God the praise.

Be the first to praise and the first to deserve praise.

The praise-life wears out the self-life.

Only those who have struck the deepest note of penitence can reach the highest note of praise.

Thankfulness is the tune of angels.

Thankfulness is the soil in which joy thrives.

A grateful mind is a great mind.

Praise is the fairest blossom which springs from the soul.

Every furrow in the book of Psalms is sown with the seed of thanksgiving.

God is pleased with no music below so much as with the thankful songs of His saints.

If you don't get everything you want, think of the things that you don't get that you don't want.

PRAYER

Cold prayers, like cold suitors, never make much headway.

The more you pray, the more the Holy Spirit will push you out into service.

A child of God can see more on his knees than a philosopher on his tiptoes.

Prayer is not conquering God's reluctance but laying hold of His willingness. (ECC 02)

PRAYER (Cont.)

Praying without watching is like sowing a field with precious seed, then leaving the gate open for the swine to come in and root it up.

God always will have to do in secret with the soul which He intends to use in public.

ECclo' Satan trembles when he sees the weakest saint upon his knees.

Our ability to stay with God in the prayer closet is the measure of our ability to stay with God when we are outside of it.

Our short prayers in public owe their point and efficiency to the long ones in private that have preceded them.

If God is not our first in our thoughts in the morning, He will be last in our thoughts all day.

To be little with God is to be little for God.

The prayer closet is the best school for Christian workers.

One can see God in everything, but we can see Him best with our eyes shut.

He who does not pray when the sun shines, knows not how to pray when the clouds arise.

God's acquaintance is not made by brief visits. He cannot bestow rich gifts upon hasty comers and goers.

Talking to men for God is a great thing, but talking to God for men is the first thing.

Prayer is a promoter of activity, for it puts one at the disposal of God.

When the outlook is bad, try the uplook.

PRAYER (Cont.)

Some go to prayer, not to ascertain the will of God but to ask Him to do that on which they have fully set their minds.

(Ecc.) Prayer means warfare; and every time we pray, we possess more of the enemy's ground.

If there was more private prayer, there would be shorter prayers in public.

Soldiers of the Lord are doing real fighting when they are on their knees.

Count it a blessing when God delays the answer to your prayer in order to enlarge your capacity to receive.

God honors no drafts where there are no deposits.

Don't pray for tasks equal to your powers but powers equal to your tasks. *Ecc (02)*

Speech distinguishes men from animals, but speech rising into prayer distinguishes the children of God from the children of this world.

In heaven's calendar the most notable days are those when human prayers move the arm of Omnipotence.

Some talk so much about the philosophy of prayer that there is no time for the practice of prayer.

Many prayers go to the dead-letter office of heaven for want of sufficient direction.

To whip the devil, fall on your knees.

Money millionaries have a poor rating alongside of prayer millionaries.

It is worth a long term in the school of Christ to learn to pray.

Jesus never has office hours or imposes a secretary between Himself and the believer.

Ea (02) He who begins the day without God makes a false start and stumbles at the very beginning.

When God has shut our mouths in argument about prayer, then He will open our mouths in amazement at answered prayer.

The people who pray in secret are ready to pray in public.

The doubtful petitioner does not offer God a steady hand in which to deposit His gift.

There needs be more fear that we will not hear the Lord than that He will not hear us.

To spend and be spent in what is called the Lord's work when the life is prayerless, is one of the devil's pet delusions.

The prayer closets of God's people are where the roots of the church grow.

In all thy prayers, let thy heart be without words rather than thy words without thy heart.

A man may pray on his knees all day, but while he preys on his neighbors he will not reach God's ear.

Satan may build a hedge about us and hinder our movements, but he cannot roof us in and prevent our looking up.

By making an errand to God for others, you'll never fail to get something for yourself.

Where prayer focuses, power falls.

Prayer is not a device for getting our wills done through heaven but a desire that God's will may be done on earth through us.

PRAYER (Cont.)

The religion of some people consists principally in praying that the Lord will provide.

He who embraces in his prayer the widest circle of his fellow creatures is most in sympathy with the mind of God.

He never rises high who does not know how to kneel.

We lie to God in prayer if we do not rely upon Him after prayer.

Prayer must not come from the roof of the mouth but from the root of the heart.

The Christian who says his prayers to men will not get answers from God.

The quickest way to get on your feet is to get on your knees.

Anchor yourself to the throne of God, then shorten the rope.

The secret of the Lord is imparted to those who have no secrets from Him.

Tarry at a promise until God meets you there. He always returns by that road.

Strength in prayer is better than length in prayer.

Power with God will be the gauge of real power with men.

Scottish preacher's prayer: "O Lord, guide us aright, for we are verra verra determined."

The only way to do much for God is to ask much of God.

Praying will make one cease from sinning, and sinning will make one cease from praying.

PRAYER (Cont.)

Pray hardest when it is hardest to pray.

God's promises are always broader than our prayers.

There are prayers that break the backs of words; they are heavier than any human words can carry.

God is constantly withholding from us things we think would be blessings but which would direct attention to ourselves instead of Him.

One cannot closet himself with the Rose of Sharon without conveying the fragrance when he goes forth.

Nothing lies beyond the reach of prayer except that which lies outside the will of God.

Prayer is more discussed and less practiced than any other doctrine.

The devil has to work hard for all he gets in the home of a praying mother.

You may have good grounds for asking, but you must first be on praying ground.

It is not enough that prayer is offered for a good object; it must come from a yielded heart.

The prayer that ascends highest comes from the lowest depths of a humbled heart.

Walk in the company of vain thoughts all the day and you will hardly shut the door upon them when you go into the prayer closet.

God cannot disappoint the desires that are of His own kindling or the hopes of His own raising.

PREACHING

Ministers - Teachers

The world has lost many a good blacksmith by their having become preachers.

When salary plays a great part with a minister, the heart plays little part.

Jonah learned more at the bottom of the sea than some preachers learn at the seminary.

The preacher is called to be a shepherd, not a sheep dog.

Preachers who are mightiest in their closets with God are mightiest in their pulpits with men.

Jesus aimed His preaching at the biggest guns in the synagogue.

When the Word of God is preached, the people take up the work of God.

Never preach a sermon until it has been soaked in prayer.

Dyspepsia has spoiled many a good sermon.

If a preacher doesn't believe in a personal devil, he cannot preach a straight sermon on salvation.

There will be no more life in the bodies of the church members than there is blood in the sermons the pastors preach.

Some preachers have a wealth of thought; others have a thought of wealth.

When a man enters Christian work for money, there is the devil to pay.

PREACHING (Cont.)

There are two fools in the pulpit; one who will take nothing from anybody, and the other who will take everything from everybody.

Get on fire from on high, and the people will come to see you burn.

There is no pulpit so vacant as the one without the message of the blood of Christ.

There is a vast difference between having something to say and having to say something.

There's a lot of preaching done that the devil likes to hear.

The preacher who does not evangelize will fossilize.

Many a preacher is dying by "degrees."

The best theology is the fruit of kneeology.

Words that freeze between the preacher's lips will never melt the hearer's heart.

Many a man has taken out a degree in the school of man without having learned the alphabet in the school of God.

Aim at the heart in your preaching; not every man has a head.

Sermons are like bread—delicious when fresh; but when a month old, hard to cut, harder to eat, and hardest of all to digest.

Christ began His ministry by cleaning the meetinghouse.

A sermon need not be eternal to be immortal.

The man who preaches the Word will not be obliged to take it all back in later years.

PREACHING (Cont.)

The most effective speakers are those whom God orders to open their mouths.

Whenever we shell the woods with gospel shot, we should take it for granted that somebody will get hit, whether we know anything about it or not.

Some preachers lambast the people because they do not pay more, when the people feel they are paying for more than they are getting.

He feeds others' hearts who speaks from his own heart.

The most spiritual preacher is the most natural preacher.

All some preachers offer the people is sentimental confections and intellectual shavings.

He is the best teacher who follows his own instruction.

The great preachers of the world are not the men who master their messages but the men who are mastered by their messages.

Your arrows must be winged with faith, else orthodoxy, wise arrangements, force, and zeal will avail nothing.

One of the curses of the ministry is utter smoothness. When a file gets smooth, it is of no account.

Some ministers who will not heed the snap of a man's finger will give heed to the snap of a pocketbook.

Let every minister, while he is preaching, remember that God is one of his hearers.

There is always danger to those who have to talk much about religion, that their religion may become that of the head rather than that of the heart.

PREACHING (Cont.)

Cultivate love for souls rather than love for preaching.

It is better to have a heart without words than plenty of words without heart.

Don't use a gallon of words to express a spoonful of thought.

If you would win the world, melt it down; don't hammer it.

If people sleep during the sermon, the preacher needs waking up.

If some sermons were for sale, they should be labeled Dry Goods and Notions.

It takes more religion to preach to one than to a multitude.

Many a preacher has lost the thread of his discourse while looking for pearls of speech to string on it.

It is all right to have a train of thought if you have a terminal.

Get so full of your subject that there is no room for yourself in the message.

PROVIDENCE

Circumstances - Luck

Beware of trusting to Providence matters which Providence has plainly entrusted to you.

The wonder is not that the great God does such great things, but that He stoops to do such little things.

PROVIDENCE (Cont.)

The most trifling matter may at times turn out to be the most important link in a chain of events by which God is helping forward the development of grand designs.

It is not given to our weak intellects to understand the steps of Providence as they occur. We comprehend them only as we look back upon them.

God's children are secure as long as He has work for them and His mighty plan strides on to its accomplishment over all the barriers that men can raise.

There is no use arguing with the inevitable; the only argument with the east wind is to put on your overcoat.

There are no accidents in God's purpose; the slightest incident may be a prime factor.

Duties are ours; events are God's.

Nothing with God can be accidental.

REPENTANCE

Contrition - Penitence

True repentance means not only a heart broken for sin but from sin.

To put off repentance another day means one more to repent of and one less to repent in.

You can't repent too soon, for you know not how soon it may be too late.

Some so-called penitential crying is only hypocritical lying.

REPENTANCE (Cont.)

Our repentance is far from being the condition of God's forgiveness.

Even our tears need washing in the blood of Christ before they can be acceptable.

The slightest sorrow for sin is sufficient if it produces amendment; the greatest is insufficient if it does not.

More disastrous than any drought in the physical world is that in the religious world caused by the dearth of penitential tears.

To grieve over sin is one thing; to repent is another.

Before God can deliver us from ourselves, we must undeceive ourselves by repentance.

If you would be good, you must first come to see that you are bad.

Late repentance is seldom true, but true repentance is never too late.

You cannot lay out money for the purchase of repentance.

A death-bed repentance at best is a weak and slender plank upon which to trust one's all.

God has promised pardon to those that truly repent, but He has not promised the power of repentance to all that sin.

It is one thing to mourn over sin because it exposes us to hell, and another to mourn over it because it is an infinite evil.

A man does not repent in order to be qualified to go to Christ; he must go to Christ in order to be able to repent.

REPENTANCE (Cont.)

From Christ comes the grace of contrition as well as the cleansing of expiation.

Do not imagine you have approved yourself a penitent by confessing sins in the abstract.

That man is not fit to be forgiven who is so far from being sorry for his sins that he goes on to offend.

There may be the most tormenting sense of guilt without any real godly repentance for it.

He who delays his repentance pawns his soul with the devil.

REPUTATION

Some get a reputation and keep it. Others get a reputation and make it keep them.

Reputation is what others suppose we are; character is what we really are.

Reputation is seeming; character is being.

Reputation is manufactured; character is grown.

Reputation is your photograph; character is your face.

Reputation is what you need to get a job; character is what you need to keep one.

Reputation is what men think you are; character is what God knows you are.

Reputation is what is chiseled on your tombstone; character is what the angels say about you before the throne of God.

REPUTATION (Cont.)

Reputation is what you have when you come to town; character is what you have when you go away.

Some men achieve notoriety and imagine it is fame.

The only reputation that matters is your reputation in heaven.

Reputation is a bubble which a man bursts when he tries to blow it up for himself.

It is easier to acquire a good reputation than to lose a bad one.

Reputation is a jewel ten thousand times more valuable than your diamonds.

An eminent reputation is as dangerous as a bad one.

The way to gain a good reputation is to endeavor to be what you desire to appear.

A just person knows how to secure his own reputation without blemishing another's.

Few are of greater worth than their reputation, but there are many whose worth is far short of their reputation.

When a man has once forfeited the reputation of his integrity, nothing will serve his turn.

There are two ways of establishing your reputation—to be praised by honest men and to be abused by rogues.

He who tears at a man's good reputation tears his flesh from his bones.

RIGHTEOUSNESS

**Character - Christlikeness - Godliness - Holiness
Purity - Sanctification**

A man who lives right and is right has more power in his silence than others have by their good words. *Ecc (03)*

He who is born of God is certain to resemble his father.

— When wealth is lost, nothing is lost. When health is lost, something is lost. When character is lost, all is lost. *Ecc (02)*

It takes more power to make a light than a noise.

Be more concerned about making a life than a living.

Christianity is not a cloak put on but a life put in.

Ecc(06) It is not great talents God blesses, but great likeness to Jesus.

—• Let the mind of the Master be the master of your mind. *Ecc (02)*

Craft must have clothes, but truth loves to go naked.

What you possess in this world will go to someone else when you die, but what you are will be yours forever.

People look at your six days in the week to see what you mean on your seventh day.

If heaven hasn't begun in you, the chances are you'll not get to heaven.

Conduct has the loudest tongue.

RIGHTEOUSNESS (Cont.)

Ecc(02) If men speak ill of you, live so nobody will believe them.

There may be a wrong way to do right, but there's no right way to do wrong.

— We are not what we think we are; but what we think, we are.

The best way to prove godliness is by God-likeness.

Many a man gets left because he didn't do right.

He who does right is a success to begin with, though he stay poor.

He who does wrong is a failure, though he enriches himself in this world.

Ecc(03) God is far more concerned about what we are than what we do.

Ecc(04) How can the world know what Christ is like until we show it what Christ can make us like?

Be an "Amen" Christian, but don't shout it louder than you live it.

Anything is wrong that is almost right.

What you are when you are not trying to be anything is the supreme test of what you are.

In the war of right against wrong, we can't afford to be neutral.

True character does not begin with self-effort but with self-renunciation.

For every look at self, take ten looks at Christ.

The way to heaven is to turn to the right and go straight ahead.

The Christian life is not an imitation of but a reproduction of Christ.

Whatever makes men good Christians makes them good citizens.

If the King is indeed near of kin to us, the royal likeness will be recognizable.

A living Christ in a living man is a living sermon.

Reckon him a Christian indeed who is not ashamed of the gospel nor a shame to it.

No beauty ever steals into the human face comparable to the delicate presence of spirituality.

One bad example spoils a good many precepts.

Those are the best Christians who are more careful to reform themselves than to censure others.

Character is what a man is while he is on his vacation.

The man who practices what he preaches is generally noted for short, simple sermons.

The straight and narrow path is the only road that has no traffic problem.

The world is full of men who are making good livings but poor lives.

The man who cannot live Christ in his home has no business preaching Christ abroad.

When in Rome, do as the Romans ought to do.

When one sells principle for popularity, he is soon bankrupt.

You are the very best Christian somebody knows.

Without consistency there is no moral strength.

RIGHTEOUSNESS (Cont.)

The most brilliant qualities become useless if they are not sustained by force of character.

Reputation is what men say we are; character is what we are before God, our Judge.

A man has no more religion than he acts out in his life.

Some people will make a cloak out of a very small piece of religion.

Be sure that religion cannot be right which a man is worse for having.

Nothing exposes religion more to the reproach of its enemies than the inconsistency of the professors of it.

It is not great preachers Gods needs so much as men and women great in holiness, faith, and prayer.

The man who lives close to God is never found bragging about his own holiness.

If you would be eminently useful, you must be eminently holy.

He only aspires to holiness who walks in the depths of humility.

The influence of a holy life is the greatest contribution we can make to the salvation of men.

The Lord Jesus received, is holiness begun; cherished, is holiness advancing; counted as never absent, is holiness complete.

The holier-than-thou attitude may be due to virtue, but it is usually caused by a poor memory.

Live the life if you are going to talk the talk.

RIGHTEOUSNESS (Cont.)

All Christians, like all Scripture, should be God-breathed.

Some people can talk Christianity by the yard who can't walk it by the inch.

How many people have you made homesick to know God?

Men who won't read the Bible will read "living epistles."

The person who professes the name of Christ and exhibits a changed life is an unanswerable argument for the truth and power of Christ.

To live the resurrection life in Christ is to lead many to believe in Christ as the resurrection and the life.

Those who live near to heaven receive early notices of God's purposes.

The world will judge our doctrines by our deeds.

SALVATION

Conversion - Regeneration

Regeneration is receiving a new life; reformation is merely turning over a new leaf.

Some spend time counting the cost of following Christ when they should consider the cost of not following Him.

If a hypocrite stands in the way of your salvation, it is because you are hiding behind the hypocrite.

In creation God shows us His hand, but in redemption He has given us His heart.

SALVATION (Cont.)

If you don't go to heaven before you die, you will not get there afterward.

God could create a thousand worlds, but He could not save a single soul without the cross of Christ.

That man is poor indeed who lives without Jesus, and he alone is rich with whom Jesus abides.

The only thing on earth a man can absolutely gain, is heaven.

Better be saved by the lighthouse than the lifeboat.

No one is qualified for heaven until he first confesses that by nature he is qualified for hell.

Calvary is God's eternal heartache for perishing souls.

Moral life belongs to all men. Spiritual life belongs only to those who are born from above.

God waited four thousand years to get a language intense enough to express our holy religion.

The gospel not only saves from hell but saves from that which takes people to hell.

The sum total of the visible universe which is passing away is poor compensation for that which is invisible and eternal.

God is satisfied with the cross as settling the sin question. We should be satisfied with what satisfies God.

Man cannot be saved by perfect obedience because he cannot render it. He cannot be saved by imperfect obedience because God cannot accept it. The only solution is Calvary.

SALVATION (Cont.)

Let *Deserved* be written on the door of hell, but on the door of heaven, *The Free Gift*.

Faith places the death of Christ between the sinner and God's judgment, and pleads His merits for those which the sinner should have but has not.

Man talks of the survival of the fittest, but the glory of the gospel is that it transforms the unfit.

Life with Christ is an endless hope; without Him it is a hopeless end.

If the way to heaven be narrow, it is not long; and if the gate be straight, it opens into everlasting life.

There are but two classes in the world—the saints and the aints.

The nearer we get to God by grace, the more we feel our distance by nature.

If we could merit our own salvation, Christ would never have died to provide it.

There is but one ladder to heaven—the cross.

A man may be almost saved yet entirely lost.

No man shall be in heaven but he that sees himself fully qualified for hell, unless grace plucks him as a brand from the burning.

We cannot ascend into God's heaven until we first descend into the hell of our own heart.

Empty buckets are fittest for the well of divine grace.

Simply clipping a tiger's claws will not make him lose his taste for blood; good resolutions and reformation cannot save a soul.

Noah's belief led him into the ark; and the ark, not his belief saved him. Christ is the ark in which we find our salvation.

A dollar can be made to do many things, but it can't be used to buy a reserved seat in heaven.

Don't think you are necessarily on the right road because it is a well-beaten path.

Men may be able to polish men, but only God can cleanse them.

There is something wrong with the man who knows the right way to take and still wants time to think about it.

You can always be sure you will hear God's voice at Calvary.

The saddest road to hell is that which runs under the pulpit, past the Bible, and through the midst of warnings and invitations.

The works of creation are admirable, providence is beyond our comprehension, but redemption is what the angels desired to look into.

Conversion may be the work of a moment, but a saint is not made overnight. Christian character is a development.

Don't expect to understand everything about regeneration. A religion without mystery must be one without God.

When one deliberately waits until old age to give himself to Christ, he is making a sacrifice to God of the devil's leavings.

If Christ is the Way, why waste time traveling some other way?

SALVATION (Cont.)

Feelings cannot connect the soul with God. It is faith that links the possessor with God, who gives salvation.

Feelings have to do with one's own fluctuating condition; faith has to do with Christ's eternally enduring sacrifice.

SECOND COMING OF CHRIST

One cannot think of the return of the holy Christ if the conscience is not at rest in the sense that sin is put away.

Live as if Christ died yesterday, rose this morning, and was coming back tomorrow.

To neglect or deny the Lord's coming is heresy; to fix a date for it is lunacy.

Those who really believe Christ is coming soon are not the ones who are fattening their bank accounts as if expecting to remain on earth forever.

The people who are most ready for Christ's second coming are those who are most interested in His first coming to save the lost.

Christ's second coming is an integral part of the gospel as much as are salvation and consecrated service. (1 Th 1:9-10).

Higher critics do not come from the ranks of those who believe in the personal and visible return of the Lord.

There is no such incentive to evangelism as an intelligent, scriptural belief in the personal, premillennial advent of the Lord.

Belief in His imminent coming is the secret spring of holiness (1 Jn 3:3).

The second advent is mentioned 318 times in the New Testament, or once in every twenty-five verses.

Satan wants the coming of the Lord to appear as an angry threat, but Jesus gave it as a choice cordial for fainting hearts (Jn 14:1-3).

The greatest message of comfort for the believer is the hope of Christ's return, for it is the undoing of all that death has done for 6,000 years (1 Th 4:18).

The postmillennialist hopes for the best; the pre-millennialist has the best hope.

The world's reformers look to the crowd; the believers look to the cloud.

The best optimism in the world is "that blessed hope, the glorious appearing of the great God and our Saviour" (Titus 2:13).

Those who believe in His visible return are not looking for the undertaker but the Uptaker.

Since His first coming became history, the second advent has been the dominant note in every prophetic strain. It is as certain to be literally fulfilled as was His first coming.

An habitual outlook toward the Lord's return fosters a spirit of preparedness which is the most potent aid to sanctification.

A Christian is defined as the one who has "turned to God from idols to serve the living and the true God and to wait for his son from heaven" (1 Th 1:9).

The Christian sacrament looks both ways, not only to the atonement in the past but onward "till He comes." At His table we are witnesses of this.

The good work which the Lord has begun in us (Phil 1:6) culminates only when He appears to "present us faultless before the presence of his glory with exceeding joy."

The prospect of His coming again in person is so ingrained in the New Testament that to believe the Scriptures as truth is inevitably to believe in His visible return.

Twenty-one times our Lord Himself refers to His return, and many of His parables concern His going and coming again and the interval between.

The second coming is the perpetual light on the path which makes the present bearable.

I never begin my work without thinking that perhaps He may interrupt that work and begin His own. His word to all believing souls is, "Till I come." *G. Campbell Morgan.*

There is not a Christian doctrine that receives more attention in the Word of God than the second coming of our Lord. It is associated with every Christian doctrine and comes in at every point of Christian life.

It is difficult to conceive that any Christian who believes that the statements contained in the Bible are divinely inspired, can deny the personal and pre-millennial coming of the Lord.

If He is coming soon, it is a cruel thing not to preach it, speak of it, sing about it, spread it.

We shall not understand Scripture unless we seek to make as prominent in our thoughts as on its pages, the second coming as the complement and necessary issue of the first coming.

If any deny the Bible to be the Word of God, then he can honestly deny the second coming.

From Genesis 3:15 to Revelation 22:20, the truth of the Lord's second coming is like a silver cord running through all Scripture.

Christianity is an incomplete, imperfect, and unfulfilled thing unless the goal of it is the return of Jesus to complete that which He began.

At the communion table we call to mind the sacrificial death by means of an ordinance which points forward to the glorious advent—"until He come."

The second coming is the climax and culmination of His work of redemption, when the body of Christ will be completed and every believer clothed with glorious immortality.

Oh, that Jesus would come while I am in life, so that I could, with my own hands, present Him with the crown of England and the Empire of India. *Queen Victoria*

To be ignorant of His coming, to doubt it, to deny it, to be indifferent to or disinterested in it, is to miss the divine equipment for the distress and pressure of these ever-darkening days.

SELF-DENIAL

Cross-bearing

The highest bidder for the crown of glory is the lowest bearer of the cross of self-denial.

SELF-DENIAL (Cont.)

The way to get rid of your cross is to die upon it. Jesus bore no cross in the resurrection.

It is not what we take up but what we give up that makes us rich.

You cannot steal quietly to heaven in Christ's company without a cross to bear.

An opportunity to sacrifice is a chance to get acquainted with Christ.

Seeking now to fit our shoulder to the cross, we shall someday find our brow fitted to wear the crown.

We may not be called upon to lose our life for His sake; but enabled by His grace, we can always deny self for His sake.

To take up His cross and follow Him is to go right on in the path in which Jesus leads and meet the suffering and shame that lie there.

Faith would soon freeze without a cross.

Since Jesus bore the cross and died on it for us, ought we not to be willing to take it up for Him?

Weak men are afraid of the shadow of the cross.

It is not enough to lighten the crosses of other people; we must bear His cross.

The Lord's church is a church of the cross, a society of crucified hearts.

Fellowship in Christ's sufferings is the qualification for sharing in His dignity.

Welcome the cross of Christ and bear it triumphantly, but see that it is indeed His cross and not your own.

He should not be weary of the cross who is sure of the crown.

SELF-DENIAL (Cont.)

The crosses we fear are heavier than the crosses we bear.

The cross is easier to him who takes it up than to him who drags it along.

We have fallen upon an evil time if we are found glorifying in Christ's cross for us, while we shrink from taking up the cross for Him.

That cross is no longer a cross, where there is no self to suffer under it.

That which we have given up for Christ is not forfeited but transferred.

He who receives scars for Christ here will wear stars with Christ there.

SELF-RIGHTEOUSNESS

Morality - Reformation

Reformation is turning over a new leaf, but regeneration is receiving a new life.

It is better to be a lame man on the right road than a self-righteous man on the wrong road.

The devil's particular delight is to get people satisfied with their own righteousness.

Many have fallen from the spot where you now stand. Trust not in your own righteousness.

It is good to be gratified but dangerous to be satisfied.

Many think if they live respectably they will go through to heaven all right.

SELF-RIGHTEOUSNESS (Cont.)

Some who write fine ethical systems can't be trusted when they go out at night.

Be suspicious of the good that wicked men can praise.

Some secure themselves in the conceit of not bringing forth evil fruit. A Christian is not defined by mere negatives.

Beware of men who speak of religion but not Christianity, and of Jesus but not the Lord.

All that morality without Christ can do for a man is give him the best room hell affords.

Some talk about being self-made men. That relieves God of a great responsibility.

There are the righteous who believe themselves sinners and the sinners who believe themselves righteous.

Moral life belongs to all men; spiritual life is possessed only by the regenerated.

God never begins at a man's fingers' ends to save him but with his heart.

The greatest sinners are those who feel sin least of all.

The goodness which thinks itself upon the summit will never toil much farther.

Morality may be the vestibule of Christianity, but it will never save a man.

Morality will be very difficult for the man who is not born of the Spirit.

Morality must accompany religion, yet religion is much more than morality.

SELF-RIGHTEOUSNESS (Cont.)

Morality is accepted of God as far as it goes, but it is not the road to heaven.

If a man wants a full knowledge of morality, he must go to the New Testament.

Aim above morality; be not simply good—be of use to God.

True morality is the fruit of salvation. To desire the former without the latter is to desire an apple without the apple tree.

With caution indulge the supposition that morality can be maintained without Christianity.

SERVICE FOR CHRIST

Efficiency - Fruit-Bearing - Work

Don't expect God to put you in a bigger hole until you plug the one you are in.

Jesus took more delight in finding a hungry soul than in partaking of the daintiest meal.

The way to get out of a humble position is to be conspicuously effective in it.

Many a little thing we cast to the ground is found to be a gem when someone else picks it up.

A loafer in the church is of no more account than a loafer on the street corner.

The man who gets on is the man who is a little bigger than his job.

A small man can make a big job shrink to littleness, but it takes a big man to make a little job grow into a big one.

Be not simply good; be good *for* something.

A helping hand in time of need is worthy a volume of good wishes.

The man who does good cannot help but love his occupation.

Count the days lost in which you have not tried to do something for others.

It is better to do one little thing for God than to promise forty things you will never do.

It is better to say, "This one thing I do" than to say, "These forty things I dabble in."

If we cannot do the good we would, we ought to do the good we can.

It isn't what we know, but what we *sow* that does the good.

You can always distrust a man whose love of humanity does not extend to Jesus Christ.

Our grand business is not so much to see what lies dimly in the distance but to do what lies clearly at hand.

Time for employment; eternity for enjoyment. This life for battle; the next for the crown.

It is a great thing to do a little thing well.

Without prayer no work is well done.

Most of our blunders come from letting our wishes interpret our duties.

Emotion is no substitute for action.

We are saved to serve, but we never serve to get saved.

SERVICE FOR CHRIST (Cont.)

No one lacks for ways of doing good—only for the inclination.

One day is as good as two for him who does everything in its place.

Expect great things from God and attempt great things for God.

Whom God calls, He qualifies; and when He qualifies, He sends.

We can measure our likeness to Christ by the range of our sensitiveness to the world's sorrow and pain.

The call of God to a piece of work is the guarantee that He will be the resource of all the strength needed.

If we reverently open God's callings, we shall find each one a storehouse of the needed strength.

Believe that there is nothing too small to do well.

There are no gains without pains; therefore, plow deep while the sluggards sleep.

Three helping each other are as good as six.

Pray till the tears come; work till the sweat comes; give till it hurts.

Men wrangle, write, and die for religion. Why don't more people live for it?

Between the great things we can't do and the little things we feel above doing, the chances are we will do nothing.

The debts we owe to God are payable to man.

God can't use anybody until he is willing to be a fool for Christ's sake.

SERVICE FOR CHRIST (Cont.)

If you are doing no good that will live after you, you are not ready to die.

God doesn't ask for preachers for the harvest—but laborers.

Nothing good ever started with the majority—one with God is enough.

It is not a sin to work for one's daily bread, but it is a sin to work for nothing else.

God measures loyalty to Himself not by expressions of feeling but by service.

Service is love in working clothes.

We shall have all eternity to celebrate the victories, but we have only the few hours before sunset to win them.

It is one of the beautiful compensations of life, that no man can sincerely try to help another without helping himself.

He who would not serve God unless something be given him would serve the devil if he would give him more.

Turn your beliefs into practice, or they will not long be beliefs.

The work an unknown good man has done is like a vein of water flowing hidden underground secretly making the ground green.

The talents with which the believer is entrusted are not to be laid up but laid out.

Train your eye to watch for other's needs and to read another's woe. Train your soul to sympathy, and your hand to helpfulness.

SERVICE FOR CHRIST (Cont.)

He who lifts another's load, soothes another's smart, puts music within a brother's soul, enters on earth into his Master's joy.

You will never be saved by your good works, but you will never be saved without them.

That man is of most use to the world who gives himself most freely to God for God's use.

One must breathe the atmosphere of the back side of the desert to be of any account to God in public service.

Even those who are qualified for great employment must not think it strange if they be confined for a time to obscurity.

The quality of your greatness depends upon what you do with that which is least.

Be sure you are growing smaller when you begin to disparage humble services.

The finest services are within the power of the poorest people. The deepest ministries find their symbols in cups of cold water, which are within the power of anyone to give.

Let every occasion be a great occasion, for you cannot tell when circumstances may take your measure for a larger place.

A stone fit for the wall will not long be left in the road.

The present moment is divinely sent; the present duty is the Master's will.

What most people need in their work is not more brains but more pains.

It is tragically possible to have a saved soul and a lost life.

SERVICE FOR CHRIST (Cont.)

It is impossible to take your pleasure here in this world and afterward reign with Christ.

A man's religion never accumulated by laying it away in cold storage.

Heaven, earth, and nature combine to take away the talent you hide under a bushel.

Some people never get religion in their hands and feet.

Get down from your roost and boost.

The biggest cemetery is where the unused talents lie buried.

The fellow who is pulling on the oars usually hasn't time to rock the boat.

Get in tune with the Infinite, but keep in touch with humanity.

Get religion in your *soul*, but let it get down in your *soles* also.

By every limit we put upon our sympathies, we become less like Christ.

The way to do a great deal for Christ is to keep on doing a little.

Be looking for something more to do for Christ, and you will keep receiving more from Christ.

No one is useless in this world who lightens the burden of someone else.

SIN

Impurity - Indecency - Iniquity - Unrighteousness

Show no mercy to little sins. Had Saul destroyed all the Amalekites, no Amalekites could have destroyed him.

Nothing so blinds men to the real character of sin as the fact it is their own.

It is little use trying to respect a man who does not respect himself.

If you want to form a tolerably true opinion of yourself, consider the thoughts of your own heart when you are alone.

The man who built the first scaffold perished on it; men are often caught in the trap of their own making.

His heart cannot be pure whose tongue is not clean.

Harboring secret sin will eventuate in open defeat and ruin.

What a man thinks when he is alone in the dark shows what he is at heart.

Sin is the greatest of all detectives; be sure it will find you out.

History begins in the sin of man and will come to a head in the "man of sin."

Evil deeds come back to roost. They may be slow of foot, but they are sure of scent and never make a mistake in lighting.

The thoughts we habitually dwell upon will eventually burst forth into action.

SIN (Cont.)

Kill that sin in your heart, or it may become your monster.

Let no picture hang on the walls of your imagination that may not hang on the walls of your home.

What hinders you more than the unmortified lusts of your own heart?

He who falls into sin is a man; he who grieves at it is a saint; he who boasts of it is a devil.

We need to ask the Lord to save us from evil hearing as well as evil talking.

You don't have to go on strike to get an increase in the wages of sin.

One who has light views of sin will never have great thoughts of God.

He who allows himself everything that is permitted is very near to that which is forbidden.

If we give soft names to sin, we depreciate the value of the blood which was shed to save us from sin.

The greatest sinners are those who feel sin least of all.

He buys honey dear, who has to lick it off of thorns.

A bad thing is dear at any price.

Sin's worst, brought to God, is no match for His grace.

The trouble with a little sin is that it won't stay little.

He who would understand the falsehood and deceits of sin must compare together its promises and its payments.

SIN (Cont.)

Christ will not live in the parlor of our hearts if we entertain the devil in the cellar of our thoughts.

Whenever a man is ready to uncover his sins, God is ready to cover them.

Every sinning soul carries within itself the necessary elements of hell.

God's sword has been sharpening upon the revolving stone of man's daily wickedness, and if man does not repent, it will speedily cut him in pieces.

There is no difference in quality between sins of omission and sins of commission—both are fatal.

Unconfessed sin breeds in its lurking place and multiplies its hateful offspring.

The first essential in all moral reformation is to call sin *sin*.

Active zeal for Christ is no guarantee of a holy life; one may be up in theory but down in practice.

Those opinions come not from God that lead to sin.

The greatest of all faults is to be conscious of none.

We can only know God's estimate of sin by the sacrifice which He has provided to atone for it.

No man can produce great things who is not thorough in dealing with his own sins.

Our greatest moral problem is the right use of leisure.

How candid we are when confessing other people's sins!

If you do not want the fruits of sin, stay out of the orchard.

SIN (Cont.)

Some sell themselves to the devil; others rent themselves out by the day.

The devil's chloroform is the denial of sin.

When a man confesses his own and not a neighbor's sin, he is not far from the kingdom of God.

You cannot keep the devil from coming down your street, but you can keep him from stopping at your house.

You won't have to institute a lawsuit to collect the wages of sin.

The flesh is the worm on the devil's hook.

It is sad that our troubles try us more than our transgressions.

Sin deceives, then defiles, then deadens.

Count on this: the wages of sin will not be lowered.

It is not the back but the heart that must bleed for sin.

Few love to hear of the sins they love to act.

Sin every day takes out a patent for some new invention.

Other men's sins are before our eyes; our own are behind our back.

Sin may be clasped so close one cannot see its face.

How immense appear to us the sins we have not committed.

No sin is small, for it is against an infinite God.

Let no man imagine he can pursue a good end by evil means.

SIN (Cont.)

The sin that now rises to memory is your bosom sin.

No man is compelled to evil; consent alone makes it his.

Use sin as it will use you; spare it not, for it will not spare you.

It is the little breaks with God that rob men of their power and usefulness.

A man may suffer without sinning, but he cannot sin without suffering.

Sin is an ill guest, for it always sets its lodging on fire.

The most expensive thing in the world is sin.

The enemy never can defeat God's people until some Achan tries to hide his sin in the camp.

Little sins are the pioneers of hell.

Every confession of sin is a fresh installment of the consciousness of God, a barrier against the further commission of sin.

To love a small sin is a great sin.

Sin is a brat that nobody cares to have laid at his own door.

More people are ready to shrink from sinners than they are from sin.

You hate sin just in so far as you love Christ.

If one has a propensity for falling into the fire, it is well to stay off the hearth rug.

SKEPTICISM

Atheism - Doubt - Heresy - Infidelity - Rationalism Unbelief

When skepticism is recognized as simply the un-ripe fruit of knowledge, it won't stand as high in the intellectual marketplace.

The fellows who don't want to believe the Bible read more about the Bible than they do of it.

Perhaps we can't prevent doubts entering our minds, but we can prevent their becoming a fixture there.

Some people are conceited enough to think God changes His plans and purposes to suit their opinions and practices.

Some men will be surprised someday to find that God knows more than they do and that He says what He means and means what He says.

He who will believe only what he can fully comprehend must have a very long head or a very short creed.

No infidel can be persuaded to go and live in a country that has no Bible.

An athiest has a reason but no hope for his reason. A hypocrite has a hope but no reason for his hope. A Christian has a reason for his hope and a hope for his reason.

The best place to kill a doubt is at the foot of the cross.

The only way to see the Light of the world is to put out your own candle.

SKEPTICISM (Cont.)

Rationalism is as old as the devil, and he was the author of it.

The genuine doubter is a man who fights his doubts, not the man who wears them as a feather in his intellectual cap.

Most of the skepticism about the Bible arises from utter ignorance of it.

It is better to dwell in the dim fog of superstition than in the rarified air of skepticism.

The certainty of the truth is not at all affected by persistent rejection of it.

Many do not want the Bible to be true, because its teachings condemn their practices.

Real doubt is looking for light; unbelief is content with darkness.

Nothing is so impenetrable to reason as prejudice that closes its eyes to evidence.

He is progressing who doubts his doubts.

Higher criticism makes for lower religion.

Doubt is hell in the human soul.

Honest doubt is the vestibule of faith.

Doubt springs from the mind; faith is the daughter of the soul.

To get rid of your doubts, part with your sins.

No one is so much alone in the world as a man who denies God.

There are few men who can't be eloquent for atheism.

The nurse of infidelity is sensuality.

Freethinkers are generally those who have done little thinking at all.

An atheist has gone one point beyond the devil: the devil believes and trembles.

Where was there ever a mother who taught her child to be an infidel?

To take away the hope of immortality is to add death to death.

When men are brought to believe that they die like beasts, they are soon brought to live like beasts.

Everything valuable has a compensating power. Infidelity gives nothing in return for what it takes away.

It is no advantage to be near the light if the eyes are closed.

Error needs artificial support; truth can stand alone.

The theories that make the most noise are the exploded ones.

A lie can be dressed up to look a great deal like the truth, but the dress will wear out.

Error will slip through a crack, while truth will stick in the doorway.

SOUL-WINNING

Confession of Christ - Evangelism - Testimony Witnessing

Be not simply a reflector of Christ: be a radiator.

The biggest piece of work a Christian can do is to find his friend and introduce him to Jesus Christ.

The leanest people spiritually are those who try to keep to themselves all the gospel blessings.

Whether you are an iron, brass, or gold candlestick, see to it that you shine for Christ.

If we mix our seed-sowing with doubt, the harvest is apt to be weeds.

The next thing to knowing we have found Him is to find someone else and say, "Come and see."

What the church needs is not a spurt, but a spirit of evangelism.

He is apt not to go to heaven who is content to go alone.

Little sentences spoken in faith for Jesus save souls for eternity.

If you witness to anyone about Christ, it will have to be while you are on earth.

Ecc(o4) The light that shines farthest shines brightest at home.

The guess-so Christians are never found among the soul-winners.

— Let your life speak for Christ, but let not your lips be silent.

There are nets that will not catch fish, because they need washing and mending.

Christ not diffused is Christ misused.

Those are the most valuable sermons where one man is the preacher and one man is the congregation.

Every man has a better right to hear the gospel once than any man has to hear it twice.

Love of souls is better than talents; grace is better than ability.

Christ never told His disciples to stay at home and wait for sinners to come to them.

There can be no greater soul-winning incentive than the hope of completing the body of Christ.

No man can be near Christ and not desire forgiveness for his brother as well as for himself.

If the devil were as lazy as most Christians, he would count his converts for each year on his fingers.

A man cannot touch his neighbor's heart with anything less than his own.

The man who shakes the tree gets the least good fruit. Handpicked fruit is the best.

Keep your light shining. God will put it where it will be seen.

Many are electric lights in church and tallow dips at home.

The torch of Christianity may be lit in church but does its burning in the shop and in the street.

He will never talk to men with real success for God, who has not learned well how to talk to God for men.

The price of shining for Christ is burning.

Zeal without knowledge is like haste to a man walking in the dark.

Many Christians are like the stream that dries up in summer and freezes up in winter.

Kindness has converted more sinners than either zeal, eloquence, or learning.

If God could speak through Balaam's ass, He could speak through you.

You can test all your big sentiment about love for humanity by what you are doing for individuals.

When you pass an unsaved man, don't forget that you may be to blame for his condition.

The surest way to drive a penitent sinner back to sin is to treat him as a reprobate.

Those witness best for Christ who say least about themselves.

It is a solemn responsibility to have in one's possession a reprieve for men under condemnation and then not deliver it.

He who would not be his brother's keeper would be his brother's butcher.

He who is pure by the blood of the Son of man should also be pure from the blood of the sons of men.

Our Lord did not call disciples to cultivate fish but to catch them.

God uses six classes to win souls: the foolish to confound the wise, the weak to confound the mighty, the base things, the despised things, the nothings, and nobodys.

Not to be out and out for Christ is to be down and out.

Reaching one person at a time is the best way of reaching all the world in time.

SOUL-WINNING (Cont.)

You can't be the salt of the earth without smarting someone.

— Too many are trying to shine for Jesus without burning for Him. Ecc (02)

Witnessing for the truth is not trench warfare. Men who stand for Christ must stand out in the open.

It is strange how some Christians can withhold from the world without compunction the best news that ever came into it.

If there is one thing that Satan is sensitive about, it is the danger of a Christian speaking of Christ to a needy soul.

Many a man who is eloquent before a large congregation is dumb before a single individual.

Christ does not say, "Go and address great multitudes," but "go and preach the gospel to every creature."

Shine like a light but do not flash at people like lightning.

SPEECH

Criticism - Judging - Scandal - Slander - Talking

About the only satisfactory substitute for wisdom is silence.

A breath of scandal makes conversation breezy for some people.

Many have gained a reputation for wisdom by imitating the owl.

139

Many a man has nothing to say and spends his lifetime saying it.

A chump is anybody whose opinion differs radically from ours.

There is so much that is bad in the best of us, and so much that is good in the worst of us, that it does not behoove any of us to talk about the rest of us.

Steer clear of the person who says of his rival, "He's all right but—"

Advice: that which the wise don't need and fools won't take.

A man is wise till he opens his mouth.

Gossip: the art of saying nothing in a way that leaves nothing unsaid.

If you say nothing, no one will repeat it.

Men who are proud of their ability to tell other men where to get off are prone to forget to tell them how to get on.

A crank is a man who has a different hobby than your own.

Be careful what you say, for you speak for all eternity.

One minute of keeping your mouth shut is worth an hour of explanations.

The willingness of the ordinary man to give advice is equalled only by his unwillingness to take advice.

Knockers are the folks who try to cover their own faults by talking about the faults of others.

It won't make your own backyard clean by talking about your neighbor's.

SPEECH (Cont.)

Talk like Robin Hood when you can shoot with his bow.

If you think twice before you speak, you'll speak twice better for it.

Eccl(x) The critic who begins with himself will be too busy to take on outside contracts.

He who relates the faults of others to you designs to relate yours to others.

It takes the whole Trinity to control our tongues.

A tongue three inches long can kill a man six feet tall.

When everybody says so, nobody knows so.

An honest man is not the worse because a dog barks at him.

A bridle for the tongue is an excellent piece of harness.

The tongue is a racehorse which runs the faster the less weight it carries.

It takes a whole brigade of saws at work to overcome the noise of one hammer.

Scandal is the shortest distance between two evil minds.

You can always tell a wise man by the smart things he does not say.

It is seldom you hear one criticized for keeping his mouth shut.

It is our own faults we most condemn when we see them mirrored in others.

Wise is the man who knows enough not to know too much.

SPEECH (Cont.)

Your neighbors' windows look a great deal better when you wash your own.

Bad news needs no special stamp to insure its prompt delivery.

Silence: the college yell of the school of experience.

Ecc(o2) Criticism: a thing that may be avoided by saying nothing, doing nothing, and being nothing.

There are three quick ways to send a message: telegraph, telephone, tell a woman.

The easiest thing in the world to cultivate is suspicion.

Few husbands would like to have their wives speak in more than one language.

He talks much who has least to say.

A ready accuser is usually a self-excuser.

Some who have no memory for good things have plenty for mean things.

Nature has given us two ears and two eyes but only one tongue, and it is surrounded by an ivory fortress; therefore see and hear more than you speak.

Resolve to run nobody down but the devil.

Guard against the leakage and loss of power that comes through hasty words.

A silent man's words are not brought into court.

Many have fallen by the edge of the sword, but more have fallen by the prick of the tongue.

A great talker is a great liar.

He cannot speak well who cannot hold his tongue.

What the child hears at the fireside is soon known at the village square.

A short intellect usually has a long tongue.

Some men pat you on your back before your face and hit you in the eye behind your back.

Discretion of speech is better than fluency of speech.

They always talk who never think.

In general those who have nothing to say contrive to spend the longest time in doing it.

To stop the tongue of slander stop your own.

Calumny would soon starve if nobody took it in and gave it lodging.

The talebearer carries the devil in his tongue and the talehearer carries the devil in his ear.

Give your tongue more rest than your eyes and ears.

Tact is merely the art of saying nothing when there is nothing to say.

Blessed is the man who, having nothing to say, abstains from giving wordy evidence to the fact.

Silent sense is better than fluent folly.

Wise is the man who knows what not to say and remembers not to say it.

The fire you kindle for your enemy often burns you more than him.

We should not only be able to talk on religious subjects but to talk religiously on other subjects.

SPEECH (Cont.)

If there is any person toward whom you feel dislike, that is the person of whom you ought never to speak.

A knocker is often a man who is in debt to the folks he is hammering on.

Many a man is not suspected of being dumb till he starts to talk.

The proper measure of a man is the size of the little things required to start him blowing off.

One can easily pick a wise man by the things he doesn't say.

Silence isn't always golden; on some occasions it may be just plain yellow.

Some folks speak as they think—and some oftener.

Good command of the language enables one to keep still.

As a man grows older and wiser, he talks less and says more.

Nothing pays smaller dividends in spiritual results than making a specialty of talking of the shortcomings of others.

The most expensive gift on earth is the gift of gab.

That which is in the well of one's heart is bound to come up in the bucket of his speech.

When a fool opens his mouth, you can see right through him.

It is better to shut up and seem dull than to open up and prove yourself a fool.

No one can criticize another justly without a prayer for divine guidance.

SPEECH (Cont.)

The mud-thrower is sure to get plastered.

You can read people like a book, but you can't shut them up as easily.

It is well, when one is judging a friend, to remember that he is judging you with the same godlike and superior impartiality.

SUCCESS

Failure - Progress

It is better to be a lame man on the right road than a good man on the wrong road.

Everybody is liable to make mistakes, but fools practice them.

The successful man is not the one who never makes mistakes but who cashes his mistake checks promptly at about 100 percent.

Impossible is a hopeful word, for it is a direct invitation to let God in.

Be not so ready to charge mistakes on others as to suspect yourself of them.

The man who calmly expects to win has already begun to conquer.

Don't allow yesterday's mistakes to bankrupt tomorrow's efforts.

You may be sure you are going downhill when your way is easy.

Going back usually begins with looking back.

It would have been better for some Christians if they had never known such great success.

When progress ceases, backsliding begins.

If you would succeed, work your tongue little, your hands much, your brains most.

Motion is back of every promotion.

There is but one real failure, and that is not to be true to the best one knows.

A man may weaken himself by always poring over his own mistakes.

The man who does not know how to learn from his mistakes turns the best schoolmaster out of his life.

It is 2 percent genius and 98 percent honest effort that brings success in any line. *Thomas Edison.*

Rubbers on lead pencils are a confession that most people are liable to make mistakes.

There is no skeleton key to the door of success.

Success comes in cans; failure in can'ts.

Nothing recedes like success.

Social success is the infinite capacity for being bored.

A conference is a group of men who individually can do nothing but who as a group can meet and decide that nothing can be done.

He who never made a mistake never made anything.

The strong aspire; the shrewd conspire; the weak expire.

One of the greatest mistakes a man can make is to think he isn't going to make any.

SUCCESS (Cont.)

It is easier to adopt the weaknesses of a friend than his good qualities.

The most earnest workers for God are those who have made enough mistakes to make them humble.

By failing we learn to go safely.

Blessed is the man who can use his stumbling stones as paving stones in the way of success.

A man should never be ashamed to confess that he has failed, which is but saying he is wiser today than yesterday.

Success is nothing but failure wearing a fresh coat of paint.

Our greatest glory consists not in never failing but in rising every time we fall.

Some people mistake the exhilaration of a downhill slide for inspiration.

The prodigal of old was not the only one who has had to lose his dollars to find his sense.

When the devil compliments you, you are a flat failure.

Being so afraid of making mistakes is the mistake some people are always making.

A real man is never beaten. Defeat, instead of being the end, is but a step in his education.

No one ever backslid on his knees.

Blessed is the man who has grace enough to own up.

You are a success if you are where God has assigned you service.

SUCCESS (Cont.)

If you would win back success, follow your back track and make things straight with God.

Wise men learn by other men's mistakes; fools by their own.

Learn to ride the horse that threw you.

If you make no mistakes, you'll never do anything. If you make too many, you'll lose your job.

The world thinks nothing succeeds like success; but Christ teaches that nothing fails like success, for it is often depraving to character (Mk 8:35).

It is good to learn of our weakness if it drives us to lean on His strength.

Any man can commit a mistake, but a fool will continue in it.

There is no failure more disastrous than the success that leaves God out of the bargain.

He that would save his life from any possibility of failure will lose his best possibility.

TEMPTATION

Often the sight of means to do ill make ill deeds done; therefore avoid the means.

Where one evil spirit tempts the busy man, a thousand tempt the idle man.

Don't think the devil is so busy in Europe that he is not watching for a chance to slip one over on you.

The man who keeps on putting his head into the lion's mouth is certain to have his breathing interfered with eventually.

The nearer you get to the cross, the hotter the battle; therefore take heed lest you fall (1 Co 10:12).

The desires of the flesh are the angleworms for the devil's hook when he goes fishing for souls.

Meddle with dirt and some of it will stick to you.

The man who flees from temptation should not leave landmarks by which he can find his way back.

The devil will steal your watch and chain, and explain it so well that you will give him your coat and vest.

We are not responsible for the thoughts that pass our door, but we are responsible for those we admit and entertain.

Wrestle with a chimney sweep, and you will need a bath.

Some fellows flee from temptation, then wait around the corner for it to catch up with them.

When the devil calls, let Jesus answer the doorbell.

The idle man tempts the devil to tempt him.

We can't keep the birds from flying over our heads, but we can prevent their building nests in our hair.

The gracious man may fall into sin, but the graceless man runs into it.

If you would master temptation, let Christ master you.

A wounded temptation may come back to you, but a decapitated temptation will molest you no more.

TEMPTATION (Cont.)

It is always at the gateway of life's greatest blessings that the devil places his picket guard for tempting.

The Christian's aim is victory, not freedom from attack.

No man can ask honestly and hopefully to be delivered from temptation unless he has honestly and firmly determined to do the best he can to keep out of it.

We are tempted, not in order to be ruined but in order to be made strong.

Temptation is a man's chance for flying his colors for Christ.

Temptations are a file which rubs off much of the rust of self-confidence.

You may not be held accountable for your weaknesses, but you are accountable for fooling with them.

It is not safe to eat the devil's porridge, though the spoon be ever so long.

Temptations that find us dwelling in Christ are to our faith like winds that more firmly root the tree.

He who would fight the devil with his own weapons must not wonder if he finds him an overmatch.

They who think they cannot wander will the soonest lose their way.

They that would not eat forbidden fruit should keep away from the forbidden tree.

Undertake some labor so that the devil find you always occupied.

TEMPTATION (Cont.)

Do not keep one eye on the temptations you pray not to be led into.

When you meet temptation, turn to the right.

The way some say, "Get thee behind me, Satan," means, "Get behind and push."

The devil never asks anybody to go farther than the next corner with him at first.

Temptation is the fire that brings up the scum of the heart.

Some temptations come to the industrious, but all temptations attack the idle.

The realization of the presence of Christ is the sovereign remedy against temptation.

Great possessions and great want of them are both strong temptations.

Every temptation is an opportunity of getting nearer to God.

A vacant mind invites dangerous inmates.

The man who in his own strength is trying to fight the devil is the man who is in greatest danger.

When you are tempted to sin, seek a place where God cannot see you.

TODAY

Punctuality - Time

Do it *now!* Today will be yesterday tomorrow.

If you do not do better today, you will do worse tomorrow.

TODAY (Cont.)

Time is the stuff that today is made of.

Every day that dawns brings something to do that can never be done as well again.

To begin tomorrow aright, you must go out today hand in hand with God.

Satan would have us try to bear tomorrow's burden with only today's grace and would dismay us with anticipation of trouble which looms in the distance.

Leave tomorrow's trouble to tomorrow's strength, tomorrow's work to tomorrow's time, tomorrow's trial to tomorrow's grace, and all of it to tomorrow's God.

Yesterday is gone forever; tomorrow never comes. God places the emphasis upon the *now of* life's day.

He who would serve God wisely and well will use today's strength only for the duties of today.

The man who is sorry he didn't do it yesterday is always going to do it tomorrow.

The only preparation for tomorrow is the right use of today.

Every hour comes with some little fagot of God's will fastened upon its back.

Take time by the forelock; he is bald behind.

Happy the man and happy he alone who can call today his own.

Tomorrow, do thy worst, for I have lived today.

Dispatch is the soul of business.

Never put off until tomorrow what you can do today.

You may as well borrow a person's money as his time.

Who loses an hour loses life.

If you have time now, don't wait for time.

You can't kill time without affecting eternity.

The wisest are most annoyed at the waste of time.

Eternity gives nothing back of what one leaves out of his minutes.

Make use of time if thou valuest eternity.

WORLDLINESS

Companions

There is no danger of conforming to the world without if you have enough of Christ within.

Lie down with dogs and you'll get up with fleas.

Wild oats will take out of your soil what no system of crop rotation can ever put back.

The path of the world seems pleasant enough if you don't stop to think where you're going.

The world's smiles are more dangerous than its frowns.

With such a starting point as the cross and such a goal as the Lord's coming, how can a Christian love the things of the world, the flesh, and the devil?

Let us fear the patronage of the world more than its persecution.

The girl who paints her face after the fashion of the ungodly, hangs out a sign "Rooms to Let."

For a sure-thing crop, sow wild oats.

The nearer you live to the world, the less power you have over it.

The pleasures of the world are but drops of honey from dying flowers.

The devil will promise you the whole world, but he doesn't own a grain of sand.

At the movie show one learns how pleasant vice is.

There are lots of Lots in the church who have pitched their tents toward Sodom.

Choose between the world and the Word; no heart can mature two crops.

The man who pays an ounce of principle for a pound of worldly popularity gets badly cheated.

The Christian is not ruined by living in the world but by the world living in him.

Some people have heaven on their tongue's end but the world at their fingers' ends.

Worldliness is simply pursuing the activities of the present life with no thought of God.

The more of heaven there is in our lives, the less of earth we shall covet.

There is no greater mistake than to suppose that Christians can impress the world by agreeing with it.

The best way to live in the world is to live above it.

WORLDLINESS (Cont.)

The most miserable people are those who make pleasure a business.

There are plenty of filling stations along the road to hell.

The "red hot mamas" they sing about didn't get that way leaning over a cook stove.

The devil's dice are all loaded.

There is no worldly pleasure without a tincture of bitterness.

Worldliness makes youth inglorious and age shameful.

Worldly pleasures trouble us in seeking them, do not satisfy us when possessing them, and make us despair in losing them.

The world itself makes us sick of the world.

The world is all title page without contents.

Trust not the world; it never pays what it promises.

WORRY

**Anxiety - Complaining - Discouragement - Fear
Melancholy - Pessimism**

Of all the troubles great or small, the greatest are those that don't happen at all.

Because you have occasional spells of despondency, don't despair. The sun has a sinking spell every night.

One cannot make good progress on the heavenly road if traveling to a melancholy tune.

WORRY (Cont.)

Nothing can make a trusting Christian blue.

You can't change the past, but you can ruin a perfectly good present by worrying about the future.

Worry: Interest we pay on trouble before it is due.

Stand on your head and the world will be upside down.

Satan covets a tired man and uses him; God rests a tired man and inspires him.

Fear is unbelief parading in disguise.

Pessimism is mental indigestion.

A mule makes no headway while he is kicking; neither does a man.

To the jaundiced all things seem yellow.

Self-pity is too small a thing in which to own a share of stock.

When you say, "I can't," you're saying, "He can't."

Beware of being a musty, dusty, crusty Christian.

The eagle that soars near the sun is not concerned how it will cross a little stream.

Fear and faith cannot keep house together. When one enters, the other departs.

"Pity thyself" is the devil's most popular sermon to all who will listen to him.

Faith is the only victorious antagonist of fear. Cast into the scale, it will outweigh a hundred good reasons for dread and despair.

The fear of being called a fool has driven many to folly.

WORRY (Cont.)

When fear knocks at the door, send faith to open it; and you'll find no one there.

Don't be too easily alarmed; the devil does a great deal with blank cartridges.

It is not the greatness of our trouble, but the littleness of our spirit that makes us complain.

Anxiety springs from the desire that things should happen as we wish rather than as God wills.

There is a virtuous fear which is the effect of faith, and there is a vicious fear which is the product of doubt.

Anxiety never yet successfully bridged over any chasm.

Anxiety is the poison of human life and the parent of many sins and miseries.

Fear secretes acids, but love and trust supply refreshing sweet juices.

Religion is no friend to supine despondencies of mind.

Do the thing you fear, and the death of fear is certain.

At the bottom of most fears will be found an overactive mind and an underactive body. We generate fears while we sit; we overcome them by action.

When you feel down in the mouth, think of Jonah. He came out all right.

The brave man is not he who never feels fear but he who advances in spite of it.

"I am an old man and have known many troubles, but most of them have never happened." *Mark Twain.*

WORRY (Cont.)

Don't be afraid of opposition. Remember, a kite rises against, not with, the wind.

Fear of failure is the father of failure.

Nothing is to be feared but fear.

Fear usually springs from ignorance.

Fear makes men believe the worst.

It is only the fear of God that can deliver us from the fear of man.

Nothing so demoralizes the forces of the soul as fear.

WORSHIP

Adoration - Communion - Reverence

Ecc (02) The man who bows the lowest in the presence of God stands the straightest in the presence of sin.

The presence of a third party may prevent the highest success in the practice of the presence of God. Get alone with God, wherever you are.

No man knows himself, who does not know how to commune with God.

If we would mirror God, our souls must be calm.

Many a man is a thousand miles away from the sanctuary when his bodily presence is there.

Christ does not ask patronage but fellowship.

No one can possibly enjoy communion with God and go where God does not go.

158

WORSHIP (Cont.)

Solitude with God is the mother country of the strong.

Our worship should not be confined to times and places; it should be the spirit of our life.

Only in the Spirit who enables us to call God, "Abba," are we able to worship spiritually.

One becomes superstitious whenever the means of worship are permitted to eclipse the Object of worship.

The same supplication that draws God's blessing down, draws the suppliant's soul up.

Inspiration in private devotion can never be replaced by perspiration in public service.

No man truly walks with God reverently, who does not walk with men reverently.

Man is the only created being who bows in humility and adoration.